AMRITAM TAVA SHUBHADINAM

AMRITAM TAVA SHUBHADINAM

A DAY OF INFINITE BLISS

By Swamini Atmaprana

Mata Amritanandamayi Center
San Ramon, California, USA

AMRITAM TAVA SHUBHADINAM
A DAY OF INFINITE BLISS

By Swamini Atmaprana

Published by:
Mata Amritanandamayi Center
P.O. Box 613
San Ramon, CA 94583-0613, USA

In India:
www.amritapuri.org
inform@amritapuri.org

In Europe:
www.amma-europe.org

In US:
www.amma.org

Contents

Dedication

Dedicated to Amma, who is the supreme teacher and the universal divine mother.

O Amma, you have come to us as a loving mother in your present form, you being an incarnation of the highest virtues. Amma, you teach us how to practice the ideals of truth, love, patience and selfless service to the world by setting an example of your life before us. This daughter dedicates "Blossoms of Blessing" to you with humble praṇāms and prayers so that by following you she will become a good child of yours.

O Amma! You are the ocean of mercy, who leads your children to attain the highest victory in their lives by your loving sweetness. You, by your loving motherly presence, train our minds to be calm and composed so that we are competent to lead a value-oriented life. To such a loving mother this daughter dedicates "Blossoms of Blessings."

O Amma! You have taken up this life by taking birth as a divine child of your parents, who were leading virtuous lives, though you are beyond birth and death. This daughter dedicates "Blossoms of Blessings" to the merciful loving mother of the whole world.

O Amma! Who throughout your life never lost inner peace and beatitude, though you had to face a series of difficult situations. O Amma, the divine child who never cried even while taking birth, to you I dedicate "Blossoms of Blessings" and pray that I transcend sorrow.

O Amma! To you I dedicate "Blossoms of Blessings," you who while being born had the complexion of Kāḷī and Kṛṣṇa and remitted rays of hope and happiness to all near you.

O merciful mother, you have taken human form to save people from the ocean of misery. You are the source of happiness to the land where you were born, spreading vibrations of everlasting joy to the whole world. At your divine feet let me offer "Blossoms of Blessings."

O Amma! Virtue personified, you from your childhood onwards have been the center of divine attraction for sentient and nonsentient beings of the whole world, and you have been the savior for all the people around you. To such a mother, let this child pray for allowing me to follow your example and advance towards perfection. Let me dedicate "Blossoms of Blessings" to you, praying again and again for the fulfillment of my life.

To your divine personality, even animals like ducks, dogs, snakes, etc, were as dear as human friends. They served and nursed you when you were in divine moods devoid of outer consciousness. Let my daily life be offered at your service as a worship flower. Praying so let me dedicate "Blossoms of Blessings" to you.

O Amma! In your childhood you went to the huts of the aged and incapacitated in your village and bathed them and provided them with all service needed. When they were hungry you fed them with your own meals and whatever food you could take from home. When you returned home you received punishment in the form of scoldings and beatings. O Amma! Let me dedicate "Blossoms of Blessings" to you.

O Amma! You could go beyond sorrow, trials and tribulations in childhood by concentrating on selfless service, seeing God everywhere and in everyone. You could overcome your own hunger by feeding those who were hungry. Let me dedicate "Blossoms of Blessings" to you Amma, while praying for a mind for selfless service.

Beloved Amma! In your childhood you could serve one and all by seeing yourself in them. You could realize that the real existence in every being is the same as your real self. I, your child, often roam about and get lost in the dark prison of "I-ness" like a madman. Amma, awaken this mind to cosmic consciousness. Let me dedicate "Blossoms of Blessings" to you. O Amma! I pray, make my mind rise above the small "I-ness" and become fixed in you, the real self.

Amma, as a child you never cared for formal education, yet you were the personification of knowledge and wisdom. Though not schooled in anything about the divine sports of Śrī Kṛṣṇa from books, you could contemplate day and night on all the unique divine plays of Śrī Bhagavān. Amma, to you, who are as effulgent as thousands of rising suns, "Blossoms of Blessings" is dedicated.

Amma, your contemplation of Śrī Kṛṣṇa's life and your continuous household work went on side-by-side. To you Amma, who are verily the personification of Bhagavān Śrī Kṛṣṇa, I offer "Blossoms of Blessings."

To this special divine child, who never failed to undertake the household chores while meditating on her playmate Śrī Kṛṣṇa, chanting "Kṛṣṇa... Kṛṣṇa..." with each breath, I dedicate "Blossoms of Blessings."

Amma, to become an example to your children, you exhibited signs of intense yearning for the beloved Kṛṣṇa, who was as if sometimes unseen by you. You were seen like a lotus flower, faded by the fire of sorrow of separation. Bless us to understand from your example at least a little bit of that love for God. And with that prayer may I dedicate "Blossoms of Blessings."

Amma! You are the personification of divinity, and you, for your own sake, require no penance or struggling to attain God. Then, why did you exhibit the scorching summer of separation from Śrī Kṛṣṇa? It was to show the world how to seek God, who is one's all in all. Today, while dedicating "Blossoms of Blessings" to you, let me pray for mental equanimity and divine love.

O Amma! Many times getting lost totally in deep thoughts of Śrī Kṛṣṇa, devoid of external consciousness, you fell down on the ground. You were nursed by the animal world–ducks, dogs, snakes and birds–all very eager to see you come back to your normal self. To such a mother who struggled so hard to reach beloved Śrī Kṛṣṇa, only to establish an example to your children, I dedicate "Blossoms of Blessings."

O Amma! You were seen enjoying the infinite bliss of Kṛṣṇa consciousness after Śrī Kṛṣṇa appeared to you as a constant presence only by becoming attracted by your intense love for him. Let this child of yours dedicate "Blossoms of Blessings" at your divine feet with repeated prostrations.

O Amma! You were immersed in the sea of divine bliss after you had the constant vision of Śrī Kṛṣṇa. Let me pray for divine love, dedicating "Blossoms of Blessings" to you.

O Amma! Śrī Kṛṣṇa, when he appeared to you, had the divine ornaments and yellow robe. He had a peacock feather in his crown, and he was playing his flute. Amma, your mind was devoid of any trace of sorrow after Śrī Kṛṣṇa's vision. Let this child pray to you to remove all sorrows from the mind and proceed towards the goal of enjoying divine bliss, and I dedicate "Blossoms of Blessings" to you.

O Amma! You had the bliss of enjoying Śrī Kṛṣṇa's presence as an indivisible consciousness behind the whole world. You enjoy the unalloyed divine bliss. Amma, let this child pray for a drop of bliss from your cup of total enjoyment. To that end, let me offer you all my life, especially "Blossoms of Blessings," the garland of the days of the first month.

In Service of Amma,
Līla Moḷ

Foreword

om̐ paramātma svarūpiṇīm̐
mātṛ rūpa manoharīm̐
amṛtānandamayim̐ tvām̐
pranamāmi muhurmuhuḥ

O my Divine Mother, the reality of all that exists, the mother of the whole world, who attracts all beings with love and makes everyone happy, let me prostrate myself at your lotus feet again and again.

This book, *Amṛtam̐ Tava Śubhadinam̐* (A Day of Infinite Bliss), unfolds a path of living, which will enable one to attain the ultimate goal of life. Every moment must be lived with the awareness of this goal. This is Amma's valuable instruction. Helping us to put this into practice in our day-to-day life is the aim of this book. I hope and pray that we are able to follow Amma's instructions. The first volume of *Amritam̐ Tava Śubhadinam̐* corresponds with the first month of the Malayāḷam agricultural year, Mēṭam̐, which falls from mid April to mid May. This volume is the first garland for Amma and includes 30 chapters for 30 days. Each chapter is divided into five sections: Praṇāmam̐ [Prostration], Prabodhanam̐ [Awakening], Prayatnam̐ [Practice], Pratijñā [Oath] and Prārthanā [Prayer].

The external act of surrendering is by prostration. Hence, the day begins with Praṇāmam̐, chanting a hymn of prostration. We become heroes when we become zeroes by surrendering to our spiritual teacher, who is none other than God in person. Surrender elevates our mind and enhances concentration. By adhering to Amma's instructions (She being our friend, philosopher and guide), our enlightened mind is then ready to face the day. The words of Amma in the Prabodhanam̐ sections are Amma's teachings. Prayatnam̐ is the narration of the various experiences of mine, obtained directly or indirectly from Amma. It is my hope that these soul-stirring experiences can be shared by the readers and made their own, if they are willing to put in sufficient effort. An oath, Pratijñā, is provided next to help better ourselves using the day's experiences as a guide. Finally, the day of life ends with Prārthanā , a prayer to Amma.

I started my āśraṁ life on the first day of Mēṭam. Being the first day of the year, this day is important, and it starts with arranging various flowers and fruits as an offering to God, and doing special worship upon opening one's eyes in the morning. Hence the first volume is named "The Blossoms of Blessings." My prayer is that the readers of this volume may improve their outlook towards life.

Before I conclude the foreword, I offer my humble praṇāms at my guru's holy feet, and my thanks to all the friends who have given their invaluable service in preparing this book. I offer this book at Amma's lotus feet, with a song of prayer for a day of infinite bliss to all:

The evening sky is glowing with the effulgence of the setting sun.

O Amma, it seems as if you are lighting the lamp
of benevolence for the whole cosmos.

The golden twilight changes its hue and turns red and ashen.
Darkening, the play of colors ends as though with
the burning of camphor and singing of Ārati.

oṁ jaya jaya jagad-jananī vandē amṛtānandamayī
maṅgaḷa ārati māta bhavāni amṛtānandamayī
mātā amṛtānandamayī

This Ārati song is sung at dusk,
Accompanied by the music of mṛdaṅga,

Blowing of the conch and ringing of bells,
In unison with the beating of drums.
Then, at night, the moonlight bathes the whole world
And Amma's children at the āśraṁ rest in the
Cosmic Mother's lap after a hard day's toil.

Amma says, "O My darling children! Sleep well and be ready in the morning to commence a fresh day contemplating, serving and loving without any expectations."

May a new day dawn—a day of infinite bliss!
A day of fullness! A day of happiness, without any fear!

In Service of Amma,
Ātmāprāṇā

A Note of Appreciation and Benediction

In the following pages of *Amṛtaṁ Tava Śubhadinaṁ*, the reader will find the heart-pourings of Swāmini Ātmāprāṇā, a devoted disciple of Mātā Amṛtānandamayī Devī. The book certainly is a subject matter for meditation for the devotees of Amma to elevate themselves to a state of beatitude. Meditation, as well as the reading of great literature, helps us to remember the Lord at all times. The illuminating texts are great assets to every seeker. Swāmini Ātmāprāṇā's effort in this direction is really ennobling.

It is the continuous contemplation of the nonchanging that leads to the calm and composed mental state, which in turn is absolutely needed for successful performance of one's duties. A day's work well-performed leads to a successful life. Well-thought and disciplined life is that which makes a good day. The present text and two other great literary works, *The Daily Thoughts and Prayers* and *The Daily Divine Digest*, published by Śrī Rāmakṛṣṇa Āśram also contribute to achieve this goal.

Ātmāprāṇā, as a medical graduate with anesthesia being her specialty, and having deep interest in spirituality came to work in the Śrī Rāmakṛṣṇa Āśraṁ Hospital in Tiruvanantapuram and worked there for a few years. Later, she joined the band of devoted disciples of Mātā Amṛtānandamayī some time in 1985. Leading a life of meditation, her ambition was to become a sannyāsinī even while working in the hospital. Amma visited the āśraṁ during one of her early visits to Tiruvanantapuram.

It was at that time Swāmini Ātmāprāṇā, who was Dr. Līla then, had the privilege of meeting Amma and was charmed by her divine personality and loving-kindness. Eventually Dr. Līla went to Vaḷḷikkāvu, and by the grace and blessing of Amma, she now dedicates all her time in service and meditation.

I am sure this first volume of *Amṛtaṁ Tava Śubadinaṁ* will be warmly received by the devotees and the devout aspirants.

Swāmī Gōlōkānanda, President,
Śrī Rāmakṛṣṇa Seva Āśram,
Kōzhikōṭu, Kērala

Introduction

Every day we wake up in a particular state of mind. Today it may be one of vigor and joy, but tomorrow it will be one of langor and gloom. Optimistic and cheerful, one day we feel as if on top of the world, but the following day we will find ourselves thoroughly vanquished and in a slough of despair. Though it is the common lot of each of us, why it happens is a puzzle, a mystery rather too hard to fathom.

One's state of mind at the time of waking is often found to influence one's experience during the whole day. On certain days our experiences throughout the day seem invariably auspicious and happy. It's as if everything we touch turns into gold. Everyone we chance to meet seems overjoyed to greet us. The path ahead seems all strewn with flowers. Everything appears radiant and sparkling, and we retire to bed in overwhelming joy and contentment. But what a shambles the next day brings us! Belying our expectation, everything turns topsy-turvy. The whole world and all the people seem to have turned hostile overnight! Daunted, defeated and humiliated at every step, we are forced to lick the dust. Cursing the day and ourselves, we refrain from all indulgences, trying in vain to seek solace in sleep. What is the rationale behind this baffling phenomenon? Why do such contradictions exist at all? Is there no remedial measure potent enough to solve it? Have we no effective means of controlling them? Or is it all just a matter of chance or providence? Is life like a sort of gambling in which we are nothing but mere pawns?

Our ancient sages, who probed the mysteries of life, have clearly explained this phenomenon. Nothing in life according to them is *casual*; everything is *causal*. Nothing ever happens without a cause, manifest or hidden. Many things that happen to us in life are capable of being modified or controlled. That does not mean there are no events beyond our control. But the fact is that we often fail to modify or control even such events as could be modified or controlled if we have the strength and will to do so. More often than not, we foolishly invite or meekly succumb to very many sorrows, miseries and disasters, most of which we can successfully avoid. Instead of blaming others, we ought to be fair enough to blame ourselves and honestly accept the responsibility. In truth, many of our misdeeds and the consequent miseries are of our own making. If we are a little prudent, we can make our lives free from a lot of conflict and tension. By being patient and wise enough, we can make ourselves more successful and happy, and enjoy life, no matter how short or long our life turns out to be.

It is common knowledge that the saplings emerge from the seed and gradually grow into trees. Likewise, it is our thoughts upon waking that determine, to a great extent, what the day will be like and what exactly the day will bring us in terms of our experiences. If we can control those thoughts, things will naturally take their own course and eventually fall more or less in place. If our thoughts are positive and pleasant, the circumstances we are in will of course be propitious. Our face will radiate the joy filling the mind so that it gets reflected on the faces of the people we meet. Our words will sound sweet and our behavior will seem nice and pleasing to others. Whatever we do in such a frame of mind is bound to be appropriate and fruitful, and the feeling of being successful will fill us with self-confidence. Thus, the self-confidence gained by success, combined with the resultant enthusiasm and vigor, as well as the loving cooperation of others, will fill the whole day with unalloyed joy. But all this depends on how we start the day.

Now, let's imagine that we start the day waking with all sorts of negative thoughts and evil designs. How inauspicious and frustrating the whole day will turn out to be! Suppose we put on a spiteful face and provoke people by harsh words or unseemly behavior. How will they react? The same way or differently? The world is like a huge mirror. What we see in it is but our own reflection. What we hear is just the echo of our own words and actions. Whether good or bad, these will unmistakably come back to us. As the saying goes, "We only reap what we sow." Thus, utterly vanquished in the day's battle, we are often destined to beat a shameful retreat, cursing the day or the stars we were born under. Is it, after all, that simple to start every day with positive thoughts? If it is, why don't we wake up with good thoughts every day? Why does our mind fail to cherish only auspicious thoughts? And why do the day's events often prove contrary to our wishes and expectations?

The only possible answer is what we call God's grace. As in everything else, it depends ultimately on the grace of God, without which we can't even have good thoughts. Our daily activities and experiences are essentially dependent on God's grace. God is the sole dispenser of the fruits of our actions. According to the law of karma, being universal and inviolable, none of us can escape the fruits of our actions. Hence, the best way to make our life worth enjoying is to whole-heartedly accept each of our experiences, bitter as well as sweet, as the gift of God.

But it is easier said than done. There again what we need is the grace of God. So, every morning when we wake up, we should make it a habit to remember God and pray for his grace. That alone is the way to make every day auspicious and thus make our lives peaceful and successful. When we make our lives holy by chanting mantras, singing God's praise, worshipping him, then his grace will naturally descend on us.

This precious book of hymns, *Amṛtaṁ Tava Śubhadinaṁ* (A Day of Infinite Bliss), written by Swāmini Ātmaprāṇā is the best ever answer to the vexing question of earning God's grace. It offers the simplest and surest means of guiding us to completely surrender to God upon waking every morning. It is the right key to unlock the grace of God. It provides us with sufficient food for thought and contemplation every day. It originates from the hymns and mantras embodied in the Vedas and Upaniṣads. Subsequently, it serves to open our eyes to the rich and profound revelations contained in them. Next follows the divine utterances of the living goddess Mātā Amṛtānandamayī Devī. What this book of hymns offers is not just ordinary food but a rare kind of ambrosial food for our daily consumption, which comprises a variety of delicious dishes, such as the Holy Mother's daily conversations with devotees, excerpts from her public speeches, and illustrative stories and parables gleaned from her spiritual discourses and the author's personal experiences and reminiscences of the Holy Mother. The contents of this book, delectable without exception, are so inspiring and edifying that they elevate our minds from all sinful thoughts. Every morsel of the spiritual fare this book provides is capable of awakening us to the ultimate realization that each and every one of us is verily immortal. We only have to have a mouthful of this nectarine food every day. It will cleanse us of all negative thoughts and feelings, and make us strong enough to start the day's journey. Before we plunge into our routine business of life, if we just care to have the Holy Mother firmly installed in the sanctum of our hearts, God's grace we are sure to have in full measure. And that will certainly bring us not just happiness and contentment, but even unexpected success and good luck.

This valuable book will certainly help a lot not only to save us from all the anxiety, feelings of insecurity and the resultant tension we are likely to feel every day, but also to transform this wayward and wasteful life of ours into a truly purposeful and fruitful one. This book is indeed a blessing, a veritable prop, a saving device we can faithfully depend on, a wonder therapy, a success mantra so potent for all to profit by. This is, in essence and tone, the very pūjā or fervent prayer we offer at every dawn and dusk. I can only pray that this book, the cumulative and tangible result of Śrī Mātā Amṛtānandamayī Devī's supreme and spontaneous grace and infinite compassion, will help spiritualize our lives and make them eminently worthy and fruitful. With utter humility and immense pleasure, let me, with confidence and conviction, strongly recommend one and all to make proper use of this precious gift offered by Śrī Swāmini Ātmāprāṇā.

P. Parameśvaran, Director,
Bhāratīya Vicāra Kēndraṁ
(Translated into English by Śrī. Evoor G. Mādhavan Nair)

|| oṁ amṛteśvaryai namaḥ ||

Mēṭam 1, April 14

Praṇāmaṁ

(Prostration)

oṁ pūrṇabrahma-svarūpiṇyai
saccidānanda mūrtaye
ātmā rāmāgragaṇyāyai
āmṛteśvaryai namo namaḥ[1]

O Cosmic Mother! You are omnipresent as the real existence, knowledge and bliss. You are a friend to all, keeping everyone company as their indwelling self. To you, I offer all my burdens, by surrendering myself at your divine feet.

Prabodhanaṁ

(Awakening)

oṁkāra nāda poruḷē
omana makkaḷē vegaṁ
omanayāyi vaḷarū uṇarū
oṁkārattil cērū

Amma says:

Amma entreats her darling children to grow up well and attain victory in life by becoming one with the supreme. Amma will destroy all obstacles on your path. All your conditionings will be eliminated and your true self will shine.

---

[1] The mantras of the Praṇāmaṁ sections come from the 108 Names of Śrī Mātā Amṛtānandamayī Devī

Prayatnaṁ

(Practice)

Through the spiritual magazine published by the āśram, Amma's call reaches the world. It came to Līla mōḷ[2] in Tiruvanantapuram. On the 14th of April, the first day of the Malayālaṁ year, Līla mōḷ arrived at Amma's āśraṁ with the intention of becoming a renunciate. In the following Prayatnaṁ sections of each chapter, she shares with the readers her daily intimate experiences with Amma.

Pratijñā

(Oath)

Every moment of my life, I will put forth conscious
effort to achieve the supreme goal. Thereby,
O Amma, let me go beyond death.

Prārthanā

(Prayer)

oṁ asato mā sad-gamaya
tamaso mā jyōtir gamaya
mṛtyormā aṁṛtam gamaya
oṁ śāntiḥ śāntiḥ śāntiḥ
(Vedic mantra)

On this auspicious day I pray:
Kindly lead me from untruth to Truth, enabling me
to transcend the illusion "I am the body" and to
merge and become one with the ultimate reality.

[2] Swāmini Ātmāprāṇā's birth name was Līla; mōḷ is Malayālaṁ for "daughter."

Kindly lead me from the darkness of
ignorance to the light of knowledge.
Kindly save me from the jaws of death.

tava sannidhiyil
samarpitāmāyōrī kaṇimalarukaḷe
tava tṛpādē karuṇayōṭennuṁ
ammē cērkaṇamē[3]

O Amma,
These little morning flowers are offered at thy altar, so
that they will be one with thy lotus feet forever.

[3] The second part of the Prārthanā sections are excerpts from various bhajans.

|| oṁ amṛteśvaryai namaḥ ||

Mēṭam 2, April 15

Praṇāmaṁ

(Prostration)

oṁ antarmukha svabhāvāyai
turya tuṅga sthalījuṣe
prabhāmaṇḍala vītāyai
amṛteśvaryai namo namaḥ

Amma, you always remain absorbed in reality. Although you undergo the different states [waking state, dream state and deep-sleep state], you do not identify yourself with them. You only witness these three states, as you have transcended them. You always emit the aura of the effulgence of saccidānanda [existence-knowledge-bliss]. To you, I bow down again and again with the prayer that you grant me your vision.

Prabodhanaṁ

(Awakening)

śṛṇvantu viśve amṛtasya putrā
āye dhāmāni divyāni tasthuḥ
vedāha metaṁ puruṣaṁ mahāntaṁ
āditya varṇaṁ tamasaḥ parastāt
(Veda Mantra)

Amma says:

"O My children! Understand that the Vedas profess the universal religion of realization of truth. You should imprint this proclamation on your mind. O darling children of eternal bliss, listen! Beyond darkness, Amma has seen the radiance of that cosmic being with the effulgence of thousands and thousands of suns. Knowing this supreme truth, we can surpass death. O children! Know for certain that there is no other way."

Prayatnaṁ

(Practice)

Having reached the āśraṁ to begin life as a permanent āśraṁ resident, Līla mōḷ waited for Amma. Amma had gone on a visit to the Kollaṁ branch of the āśraṁ with the āśramites and was, therefore, physically absent from the āśram. Līla mōḷ was feeling rather lonely. Fortunately, she had a copy of the booklet *The Amṛta Sūtras*, which she began to read. She felt as if Amma was personally speaking to her. After enjoying this indirect conversation with Amma, she started contemplating a soothing experience she had regarding Amma's omniscience.

Līla mōḷ recollects:

Last September, during Amma's birthday celebrations, I couldn't go to Amma's āśram. I prayed to Amma, "I am so sad that I can't take leave from my work and come to you now. If you are omniscient, you must be aware of this. Kindly enlighten me of the various programs of the day through someone." On the very next morning, this prayer was answered most mysteriously.

I happened to be in the office of the hospital where I was practicing as a doctor. To my surprise I heard one devotee of Amma conversing with the swāmiji who was the hospital's president. I remembered that this revered swāmiji had been invited to preside over the public meeting during celebrations and to release the first copy of Amma's āśram's monthly magazine. The swāmiji and the devotee talked for quite some time and I was thrilled to hear some of their conversation because it included all the details of their experiences in the āśraṁ the previous day.

My heart was filled with an ineffable joy, which Amma had given me by fulfilling the small wish of this little child of hers. I became fully convinced that this was Amma's divine way of answering my prayers, which in turn awakened in me the irresistible feeling of the Divine Mother's omniscience, love and compassion.

Pratijñā

(Oath)

I will put forth constant effort to think of God. Directly experiencing God, I shall be in bliss every moment.

Prārthanā

(Prayer)

oṁ bhūr bhuvaḥ svaḥ
tat saviturvareṇyaṁ
bhargo devasya dhīmahi
dhiyōḥ yō naḥ pracōdayāt
(Gayatrī Mantra - Bṛhadāraṇyaka Upaniṣad)

Amma! Your children are praying from the depths of their hearts, rendered pure through constant meditation upon you. You are the bestower of supreme knowledge. Kindly bless us with a sharp intellect to know you.

tava tiru nāma rūpa smaraṇayil
nirantaraṁ aliyān
kotikoḷḷukayāṇennuṭe cittaṁ
ariyukillē nī
aṇayān tāmasamentini collū

agatiyil kṛpa coriyū
arivinnuravē parama prēma kaṭalē arivēkū

Amma! Today my mind is yearning to meditate upon you ceaselessly. Are you not aware of this? Why this delay in coming to me? Kindly come and bless this child. You are the source of all divine knowledge and supreme love. Be kind enough to bestow upon me the wealth of knowledge and bliss.

|| oṁ amṛteśvaryai namaḥ ||

Mēṭam 3, April 16

Praṇāmaṁ

(Prostration)

om sajātīya vijātīya svīya bheda nirākṛte
amṛteśvaryai namo namaḥ
amṛteśvaryai namo namaḥ

O Amma! You are beyond the superimposition of categorizations created by the mind. You are the mother of the universe and can love one and all equally. Kindly bestow upon me an intellect wherein the concept of "I" and "you" does not exist. Otherwise, my life verily becomes a hell. Kindly bless me with unity, love, strength and peace.

Prabodhanaṁ

(Awakening)

uttiṣṭhata jāgrata
prāpya varān nibōdhata
kṣurasya dhārā niśitā duratyayā
durgaṁ pathastat kavayōvadanti
(Kaṭhopaniṣad, 1-3-14)

Amma says:

"Dear children, 'Arise! Awake' is the clarion call of the Vedas. Find the ones who have realized the truth and learn from them. The great ones have proclaimed that the spiritual path is like the blade of a knife: sharp and narrow and very difficult to tread upon. These sages are the incarnations of love and compassion. They awaken one and all in a roaring voice akin to that of a lion, but which is at the same time sweet and soothing. My children, follow them and awaken to the supreme truth."

Prayatnaṁ

(Practice)

Līla mōḷ was waiting at the āśraṁ for Amma's return from Kollaṁ lost in thoughts of Amma...

I came to Amma for the first time after several days of waiting and weeping for her. I was the sole full-time anesthesiologist in the hospital. One day Dr. Devaki arrived. She was kind and loving like an elder sister, but nevertheless very strict. She was very keen and determined to take me to meet Amma. Having arranged a program in Koṭṭayaṁ for the following day, she was on her way to the āśraṁ to accompany Amma to the venue.

Naturally, I couldn't take leave from my day's work. I completed my routine work and then I was suddenly inundated with an influx of emergency caesarean-section operations. How could I even suggest that I had to leave? I had to anesthetize the mothers undergoing surgery.

Dr. Devaki was repeatedly calling me on the phone. Around 10:00 at night, she came personally to take me along with her. Feeling so free with me, she said firmly, "You have to get into the car right now." I had just finished all the caesareans, but I still needed someone to cover for me. I had one option. I had a senior part-time colleague who was like a teacher to me. Although he was elderly, he was very energetic. Moreover, he was also very loving and helpful. I thought I would drop in on him and ask him to cover my shift. Many times on our way to his home, I hesitated and almost turned back, but Dr. Devaki urged me on and finally we reached his place. Luckily, the doctor was still awake, and he made it possible for me to leave.

I never slept that night. We were in such a hurry to reach the āśraṁ because we wished to see Amma before the bhāva darśan concluded. When we reached the āśram, it was very late at night. Our wish was not fulfilled, as bhāva darśan was already over. Though our eyes couldn't see Amma during bhāva darśan, we still experienced her darśan.

Pratijñā

(Oath)

O Supreme Self! O Mother of the Universe! During
times of pain and sorrow, whether in poverty or
affluence, in all situations of both happiness and
misery, your memory will not fade away.

Prārthanā

(Prayer)

tejosi tejomayi dhehi
vīryamasi vīryaṁ mayi dhehi
balamasi balaṁ mayi dhehi
manyurasi manyuṁ mayi dhehi
mahosi maho mayi dhehi
sahosi saho mayi dhehi
(Vedic mantra)

You are the supreme knowledge; bestow upon me knowledge.
You are the supreme courage; make me courageous.
You are the supreme strength; make me strong.
You are the great cosmic mind; bless me with a good mind.

You are the greatest; raise me to your status.
You are the greatest in forgiving; forgive me, O Amma.

ōrō nimiṣavuṁ eṇṇiyeṇṇi
tīrunnitennuṭe janmaṁ ammē
ālamba hīnayī paitaliṅu
kēṇiṭunnammaye kāṇuvānāy
saccidānanda svarūpiṇiye
māyāmahārṇava tāriṇiye
āśrita duḥkha nivāriṇiye
ammayē kaṇuvān kēnitunnu

O Amma! I am counting every moment and waiting for you. I wonder if my life is about to end. I am without any companion. How can I remain alone without meeting you? O embodiment of consciousness, existence and bliss! O mother who takes us beyond this ocean of illusion, who has come down to redeem us from this sorrow and delusion, come to me without any delay!

|| oṁ amṛteśvaryai namaḥ ||

Mēṭam 4, April 17

Praṇāmaṁ

(Prostration)

oṁ vāṇī buddhi vimṛgyāyai
śaśvad-avyakta vartmane
nāma-rūpādi śūnyāyai
amṛteśvaryai namo namaḥ

O Divine Mother! You are the embodiment of the highest knowledge, which is beyond all words and thoughts, names and forms. I offer my praṇāms on this beautiful morning.

Prabodhanaṁ

(Awakening)

tat viddhi prāṇi pāte na
pāri praśnena sevayā
upadekṣyantite jñānaṁ
jñāninaḥ tatva darśinaḥ
(Bhagavad-Gītā, 4-34)

Amma says:

"One must experience that supreme knowledge that is inexpressible and beyond thoughts. That is the goal of life. Those who have this knowledge are the great spiritual teachers. Seek such realized souls. Offer your mind, body and soul at their lotus feet and serve them wholeheartedly with love. They will bless you with the direct experience of supreme knowledge."

Prayatnaṁ

(Practice)

Still sitting in front of the shrine and waiting for Amma's return, Līla mōḷ was absorbed in sweet memories of the first day that she met Amma.

Līla mōḷ recollects:

The very first time I came to Amma's āśram, it was night. My friends and I were taken to Amma's darśan hut and were allowed to rest there. How fortunate we were! My friends could sleep very well, but I was not at all in a mood to sleep. On the wall of Amma's little hut was a small photo of her beautiful and sacred feet. Those divine feet made an imprint on my mind and filled my heart with a special feeling. The floor of the hut was filled with sand over which a mat had been spread for us. These were new experiences for me. I was eagerly waiting for the break of dawn when I could meet Amma.

The āśramites were chanting the *Lalitā Sahasranāmaṁ*, the Thousand Names of the Divine Mother. They were up very early in the morning and had finished their morning routine. After the chanting, the āśramites were getting ready for traveling to Kōṭṭayaṁ for Amma's program. I was meditating, sitting in front of a portrait of Amma. I knew that at that time Amma might come by that way. Someone came and informed me "Amma is sitting in the office. She is calling for you." Running, I quickly reached the office. My three companions were already sitting near Amma. I wished to become as innocent as a newborn baby when I offered myself at Amma's lotus feet. With tears of joy in my eyes and my heart full of divine emotions, I sat near Amma.

Dr. Devaki, Dr. Kamalam and I were the three ladies, and the man in our group was an engineer by profession and a devotee of Swāmi

Abhedānanda. Amma held each of us in a loving embrace, as a mother would do to her children. Observing this, I felt that this was very special for a young lady like Amma. I thought, "Amma has verily crossed the barriers of difference in gender, age, etc."

Dr. Devaki was a devotee of Śrī Kṛṣṇa, and the engineer who was driving us in his car was a devotee of Goddess Kāḷi, the terrifying aspect of the Divine Mother. Amma was speaking about the motherhood of God with a sweet, unique smile. Amma said to Dr. Devaki, "O my daughter, you are scared of Kāḷi? Is not Kāḷi our Mother? Why are you afraid of her? Damayanti Amma [Amma's biological mother] was also scared stiff when she heard the word 'Kāḷi.' She believed that Kāḷi would kill us with her sword and trident if she got angry. This is a big joke for Amma. No matter what Amma said, Damayanti Amma's fear would not disappear."

While I was pondering over these sweet memories, a brahmacārī from the aśraṁ came and asked me to have my food and arranged for my accommodation. Amma's father also spoke to me and enquired after me. This interruption turned my mind to the quiet relaxed atmosphere of the āśram.

Pratijñā

(Oath)

Life is nothing but a journey. Wherever I may be sometimes the continuity of the journey is broken and I am left idle. Wherever I may be, I will not waste even a moment. I will always think of my duties in life and remember the great advice "Do now what you want to do today, and do today what you want to do tomorrow."

Prārthanā

(Prayer)

bhadraṁ karnebhi srunuyamadevā
bhadraṁ paṣyemākṣabhiryajatraḥ
sthirairangaistuṣṭuva sastanubhiḥ
vyaṣema devahitam yadayuḥ
svasti na indro vruddhaṣravaḥ
svasti na puṣa viśva-vedaḥ
svasti nastakṣaryo arishtanemiḥ
svasti no brithaspatidadhatu
oṁ śāntiḥ śāntiḥ śāntiḥ
(Īśāvāsya Upaniṣad, Kṛṣṇa Yajurvēda)

May I hear goodness with the ears, see goodness with the eyes. May I have a healthy body to do goodness in the world. May I enjoy peace and happiness, O supreme benefactor of the world.

hrīṁkāra saubhāgyasad bījaṁ mūnnuru
taṅīṭumuttama mantrattāle
sēvyayāṁ ambikē vēdārttha lakṣyamē
āvatō marttyarāl ninne vāzhttān
entellāmōthunnu ñānennālokkeyuṁ
santataṁ nin stutiyāyiṭaṭṭē
sañcāramokkeyumammē pradakṣiṇa
sañcayamāyiṭṭuṁ tīrnniṭaṭṭē
saṁvēgamokke namaskāramāyiṭṭuṁ
dēvi nin prītikkāy tīrnniṭaṭṭē
ammē namaskāraṁ ammē namaskāraṁ
ammē namaskāraṁ ennumennuṁ
(Saundarya Laharī, Malayāḷaṁ translation)

O Divine Mother, you are pleased when worshiped with the mantra in which hrīṁkāra is repeated three times [Śrī Vidyā Mantra]. How can you be praised by words, you who are the goal indicated by the Vedic mantras? I pray to you to make all my words in praise of you; my footsteps must be in circumambulation of you. O Amma, may I prostrate myself at thy feet.

|| oṁ amṛteśvaryai namaḥ ||

Mēṭam 5, April 18

Praṇāmaṁ

(Prostration)

oṁ śūnyakalpa vibhūtaye
amṛteśvaryai namo namaḥ
amṛteśvaryai namo namaḥ

O Universal Mother! Your name is my supreme wealth. You possess the whole world, yet possess nothing. I offer my humble praṇāms at your lotus feet on this divine morning. Abandoning the little attractions of the world, I have come to depend upon you for everything.

O Amma! You know what your children need and you never hesitate to fulfill their needs. O Mother! I humbly bow down to you again and again.

Prabodhanaṁ

(Awakening)

vipado naiva vipadaḥ
sampado naiva sampadaḥ
vipad vismaraṇaṁ viṣṇoḥ
sampad nārāyaṇa smṛtiḥ
(Subhāṣitaṁ)

Amma says:

"O My darling children! Look at that man who is walking on the road. He is stopping there and stepping backward. He is cursing!

Now he is looking around and is calm again. His face is beaming with a smile. Taking a thorn that has pricked him, he kisses it and murmurs, 'O! If you had not pricked me and caused me pain, I could have continued walking unaware and perhaps fallen into a deep pit. I was forgetful of myself, God and my surroundings and was lost in some unnecessary thoughts. O God! You have saved me; I could have lost my life!' This man has realized that the little unfavorable event on the road was actually God's boon to him.

"Once a man bought a lottery ticket hoping to become a millionaire. One fine morning after bathing, he was in front of the mirror combing his hair. At that time, he received a phone call. He had won the first prize in the lottery amounting to 50 lakhs (Rs. 5,000,000). He could not believe his good fortune, and his weak heart failed him. Alas, he fell dead. According to most people, death is the greatest disaster, and it had overtaken him despite his being a millionaire.

"My children, what should you learn from this? It is God and godly qualities that are our greatest wealth. If you have this wealth, you have everything. You can face the worst situation easily with the remembrance of God. Now, understand that forgetfulness of God is the greatest misery. The constant remembrance of the Almighty is our real wealth. You can see many illustrations of this truth in the scriptures. The best among them is the story of the great devotee, prince Prahalād, which Amma encourages to read. O my children, depend upon God always. Amma is with you."

Prayatnaṁ

(Practice)

Amma's spiritual messages from the āśraṁ magazine engaged Līla mōḷ's mind while she was waiting alone for Amma in front of the small temple. Amma had bestowed spiritual experiences upon her that were like a cool shower to her mind. The heat of the midday sun and the dreary sitting did not affect her at all. She was thinking...

On the first day that I met Amma, the four of us were boarding a pole-boat along with Amma and the āśramites. Dr. Devaki was afraid of the journey. Amma gave her a helping hand while she was climbing into the boat. I then said to Amma, "You are the one who takes us across the ocean of life. I am reminded of a song from *The Gospel of Śrī Rāmakṛṣṇa*. Amma do you like that song?"

Amma said, "Yes, yes. Amma is very fond of that song. Can you sing?"

I started singing:

samsāram-ākuṁ mahābdhiyil-en nauka
muṅgān tudaṅgukayallo

When I finished singing, Amma said, "My daughter, Amma sings it in a different way," and she started to sing:

ennūṭe jīvita nauka bhavābdhiyil
muṅgukayāṇammē muttuṁ
māya vaḷarttuṁ koṭuṅkātturūkṣamāy
ūtukayāṇente cuttuṁ

In the ocean of this worldly existence, my boat of life is sinking.
The power of illusion is storming around me.

As Amma was finishing the song, our unique boat journey took us across the backwaters and the heavenly sight of the coconut groves was at a distance. Everyone was in a hurry to jump out of the boat and to enter the āśraṁ with Amma.

The engineer and I were walking on the road behind Amma, and I was looking at her, forgetting everything else. Previously, while we were getting into the boat, Amma had handed me a copy of *Bhajanāmṛtaṁ* [a book of bhajans published by the āśram]. She had enquired, looking at Dr. Devaki and pointing to me, "Can she not get leave for two or three days to come here again?" And during the boat journey Amma had asked me several times "O my child! Can you not come with us for the program?"

I was very sad to hear this because I was not in a position to say yes. I said to Amma, "Amma, I cannot take leave this time. I am the only regular anesthesiaologist. Also, this is Christmas vacation time. Many patients are waiting for surgery. When I return, I will have to immediately step into the operating theater and start working."

I was standing on the road looking at Amma sitting by the window. Amma told me, "Amma knows that you have resigned your government job and have come to Śrī Rāmakṛṣṇa Āśraṁ Hospital in Tiruvanantapuraṁ, where you are working now, looking for a realized spiritual teacher. Your wish is not yet fulfilled." I didn't answer. My mind had reacted three times in a slightly negative way to the statements Amma made on the way to the āśraṁ van:

First, when Amma had enquired, "Can she not get leave for two or three days to come here again?" my mind had doubted the possibility of obtaining leave.

Second, when Amma had asked, "Can you not come with us for the program?" my mind had murmured, "Why should I come for bhajans? Isn't it better to do my duty at the hospital?" Of course I hadn't yet had a direct experience of the nature of Amma's programs.

Finally, when Amma had said that I hadn't yet found a realized spiritual teacher, my mind had responded, "I have got a good spiritual teacher and a mantra from him, and a beloved deity." I then couldn't realize that what Amma actually meant was not just an ordinary spiritual teacher but the highest possible one, whom now fortunately I have come to know in her.

Amma started the journey to Kōṭṭayam. The engineer and I got into the car. My first thought was, "I have offered my mind, intellect and my whole life to Amma and have turned into a newborn baby in Amma's arms, then why did I fail to hold on to her without any mental deviations?" Now the only option left was to remember Amma constantly by reading Amma's sayings from the booklet and singing bhajans from the *Bhajanamṛtam*. Before we started the journey, Amma, the āśramites, and the four of us had not even had water to drink. In the car, my companion fetched me some bananas for breakfast.

Pratijñā

(Oath)

During unfavorable situations, I shall never deny God or curse anyone. I shall, with a calm and composed mind, remember God and get over the worst calamities in life.

Prārthanā

(Prayer)

kavitvavārāśi niśākarābhyāṁ
daurbhāgya dāvāṁbūda mālikābhyāṁ
durīkṛtā namra vipattatibhyāṁ
namo namaḥ śrī gurupādukābhyāṁ
(Gurupāduka Stotram)

Amma! You are the supreme spiritual teacher. I bow down to you again and again, and pray for strength of mind to remember you always in my life. Amma, kindly bless me with the strength to face all adverse situations in life.

kūriruḷ kūmpāramāṇente cuttiluṁ
ñānatilāndupōṁ munpē
ammatan tantiru nāmamāṁ kayilī
ponmakaḷ keṭṭippiṭikkuṁ

Amma! I am engulfed by the growing darkness of dangers.
Before I am lost, I shall hold onto you.
O Amma! Kindly save me.

|| oṁ amṛteśvaryai namaḥ ||

Mēṭam 6, April 19

Praṇāmaṁ

(Prostration)

oṁ ṣaḍaiśvarya samudrāyai
dūrī kṛta ṣaḍūrmaye
amṛteśvaryai namo namaḥ
amṛteśvaryai namo namaḥ

Amma! you are an infinite ocean of godliness. Aiśvarya, vīrya, kīrti, śri, jñāna and vairāgya (sovereignty, valor, fame, auspiciousness, knowledge and dispassion) are embodied in you. I humbly prostrate at your lotus feet.

This worldly existence goes through six states: birth, existence in the body, growth of the body, experiencing constant changes in the body, deterioration of the body and death. I am weeping and wailing under the weight of worldly life. You are my only savior.

Prabodhanaṁ

(Awakening)

śānto mahānto nivasanti santaḥ
vasantavat lokahitaṁ carantaḥ
(Vivēka Cūḍāmaṇi)

Amma says:

"My children, the great gurus have realized their oneness with God and have transcended the three factors of sorrows in the world: sorrow from selfish reactions, sorrow from fellow beings and sorrow from the cosmic powers. The great ones do not expect anything from the world. They are bound only to serve the world and reveal the path of dharma [duty or righteousness]. They can be compared to the spring season. It comes uninvited at the right time and adorns the whole earth with flowers and fruits, serving the world selflessly. It is like a beautiful bridge between the biting cold of winter and the scorching heat of summer, and everywhere there is happiness and fulfillment. Of course, the spring season comes to an end, but the gurus continue even after their demise. We have to seek out these gurus. We must follow them and listen to them. Ordinary people are like the ship in the harbor that come and go—nothing afterwards. Today my children, be aware of this truth and beware of the world and lead a life accordingly."

Prayatnaṁ

(Practice)

Līla mōḷ recollects:

After I returned to the hospital, having had my first darśan with Amma, many enquired about her. How could I answer? Can the candle light show the sun?

I told my colleagues at the hospital that Amma looked like any one of us. She didn't display anything supernatural. I did not feel like mentioning the divine experiences that Amma had blessed me with.

While crossing the backwater at night, I had a transitory experience of the One Reality behind these manifold phenomena in nature. It was when I happened to see a bright electric lamp over the backwater casting its reflection on the water. When I looked at it for a while, the light and its shimmering reflection below became one, creating the impression that the water was nothing but light. This impression immediately lifted my mind to the light of knowledge of the supreme reality. The material world disappeared and the supreme light shone within me. This was really Amma's blessing. The glittering backwater, the all-pervading space and the lamp—which was revealing all this—disappeared for the time being. In a while, we reached the other side of the backwater and soon I became my former self.

Amma seemed to me to be the lamp in the dark path of my life. Amma was a big magnet to the iron filings within me.

"Tell me, did you meet Amma in the āśram? Why are you not talking?" was my friend's question again. That day I explained to her two impressions I had gathered regarding Amma.

When four of us—Dr. Devaki, Dr. Kamalam, Dr. Devaki's engineer friend and I—met Amma in the āśram office, she had embraced us without any sense of difference. This was very unusual for a young lady and a fresh experience for me. I understood that Amma is beyond the ideas of gender, age etc, like a good mother. Afterwards, Amma came to the front yard of the āśram. I was near her. While talking to me, Amma continuously chanted "Śiva, Śiva" and softly touched my heart with her tender hands. I noted that Amma was looking at my sāri, which had certain designs on it. I explained to Amma, "You know that I am coming to you straight from the operation theater—without anything in my hand—to you, Amma! Usually I wear a handwoven white sāri with a border. This sāri belongs to Dr. Devaki, which she gave me to wear this morning."

Amma's answer was, "O my daughter, you could have asked Amma. Amma has kept clothes for you here." Hearing this, I was wonderstruck. I was also feeling a little perplexed. Did I take undue freedom with Amma, who would be my guru?

Amma's continuous chanting of the Śiva mantra and the unique way she received her children attracted me to her on the first day.

With these words I finished the narration of my experiences to my colleagues in the hospital.

Pratijñā

(Oath)

In the scorching summer of life, the spiritual teacher comes like spring. I shall fulfill my life by taking refuge in my guru.

Prārthanā

(Prayer)

gururbrahmā gururviṣṇuḥ
gururdevo maheśvaraḥ
guru sākṣāt param brahma
tasmai śrī gurave namaḥ
(Guru Gītā)

O Amma! The greatest of all gurus! As Brahmā, you give a second birth to your spiritual children. As Viṣṇu, you bestow upon us all that is needed for our spiritual growth. As the great Śiva, you take away the negative qualities from your children. Pūrṇa-brahma-svarūpiṇī, you are the supreme Brahman, and I take refuge in you. Kindly bless me with supreme devotion to you, who are my guru.

guru-caraṇa śaraṇāgatarmakkaḷ
guru-caraṇa sēvanaṁ jīvanaṁ
guru-caraṇāṁbuja prēma bhakti
ammē śrī sadgurō makkaḷkkēkū

Amma! Your children have you as their sole refuge. Your service is the whole aim of life. O Amma! I pray for love and devotion to you at the end of this day.

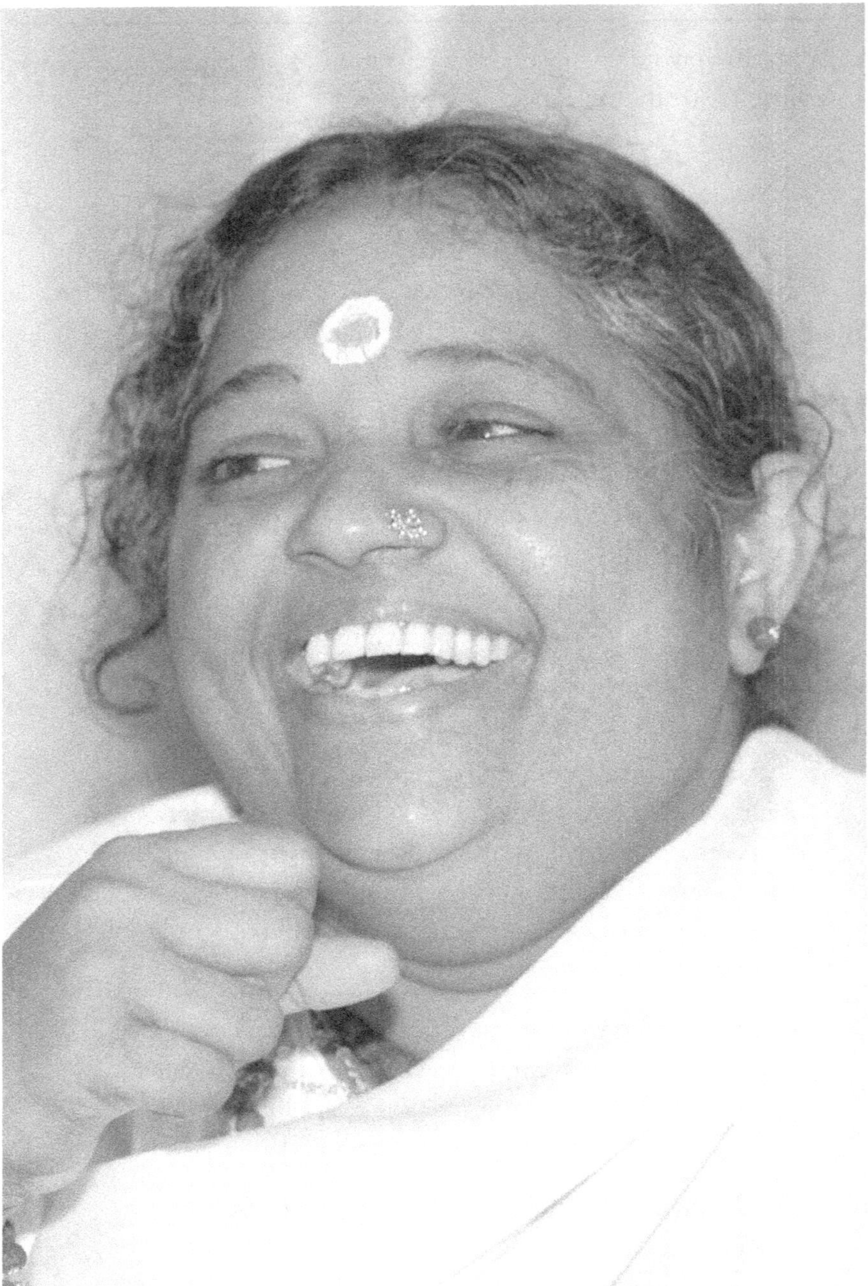

|| oṁ amṛteśvaryai namaḥ ||

Mēṭam 7, April 20

Praṇāmaṁ

(Prostration)

oṁ nitya prabuddha saṁśuddha nirmuktātma prabhāmuce
amṛteśvaryai namo namaḥ
amṛteśvaryai namo namaḥ

Amma! You are the all-pervading omniscient reality.
Amma! Kindly enlighten my intellect so that I
become increasingly pure and blissful.
Amma! You are the personification of purity
and incarnation of eternal bliss.
Please be compassionate and accept my humble praṇāms
at your lotus feet on this auspicious morning.

Prabodhanaṁ

(Awakening)

etat ālaṁbanaṁ śreṣṭhaṁ
etat ālaṁbanaṁ paraṁ
etat ālaṁbanaṁ jñātvā
brahma loke mahīyate
(Kaṭhopaniṣad, 2-1)

Amma says:

"My dear children! Any expectation you have regarding this world is bound to result in frustration. Amma has no doubt about this truth. Your experiences also reveal this fact. At present, you may be under the false impression that your friends, relatives, parents, spouse or children will always love you and be there for you. But, wait and see. Even your so-callded "nearest and dearest" will turn away from you if the circumstances are right. Their so-called "love" can easily become hatred. Of course, they are not at fault. They have not attained the necessary qualifications for selfless love—love that expects nothing in return. That is why Amma is asking you to seek the highest power of selfless love, which is the Divine Mother's power and love.

"The Śrutimātā [Sarasvatī Devī, the Mother of Knowledge] reminds us of the highest form of love and life. The eternal effulgence of the absolute love, knowledge and existence is shining within us constantly, but what are we doing? We are constructing an opaque wall between ourselves and God and then denying the existence of God. It's all nonsense! If you close your eyes and deny the existence of the radiant, life-giving sun, it is you who are the loser. Likewise, if you deny God, who is the life-giving force of the world, you become a living corpse.

"This morning, open your eyes. Come out and see the whole world filled with divine light. Look at the sun and chant the Gayatrī mantra 108 times and pray to God to illumine your intellect. Mother Gayatrī will certainly bless you."

Prayatnaṁ

(Practice)

The golden twilight appeared tranquil in the horizon of the west. The setting sun looked like an auspicious lamp lit in the evening and placed by the Divine Mother of the Universe. The little temple in Amma's āśraṁ was bathed in the evening light of red rays of kuṁkum and then the grey shades of sacred ash finally merged into whiteness as if in ārati, concluding the worship with flames of camphor.

Līla mōḷ was totally awed by the colors and asked a brahmacāriṇī, "The sea is very nearby, is it not?" She replied, "Yes, it is very near. If you climb on that stone, you can see it."

Līla mōḷ thought it would be better to enjoy the presence of the sea in Amma's company when she came back. She thought, "If Amma was here, I could have enjoyed her singing. Anyway, Amma will be coming back soon." She was happy to wait for Amma.

Līla mōḷ remembered the packet of fruits that she had purchased at the bus station for offering to Amma. She looked for it and realized that she had left it where it was bought.

This was Amma's play. (Later she could hear Amma's consoling words that Amma expects nothing from her children. She is ever ready to receive the sorrows and miseries of her children. "The mother who has given birth to you, my children, may look after your needs in this lifetime, but this mother's aim is to bestow eternal happiness to you.") She heard Amma's words inwardly, "Offer yourself, offer yourself to me and don't worry about the fruits." Līla mōḷ no longer had any regrets about the lost offering. When will Amma come? Midnight was approaching, and in the bright moonlight the tender leaves of the coconut trees were dancing, singing the peace-giving words of the śānti mantra, "Amma will come... , Amma will come... Amma will come..." She thought she could rest and relax in Amma's lap when Amma came.

Pratijñā
(Oath)

Life is a long waiting for God. Bearing this in mind I shall engage in all my day-to-day activities and keep hopes for a better tomorrow upon awakening.

Prārthanā
(Prayer)

natāyayoḥ śrī patitāṁ samiyūḥ
kadācidapyāśu daridra varyāḥ
mūkāśca vācaspatitāṁ hitābhyāṁ
namo namaḥ śrī gurupādukābhyāṁ
(Gurupādukā Stotraṁ)

You are Śrī, the Goddess of Wealth, and will certainly provide for all the material needs of the devotees. To such a mother, I prostrate again and again.

candrikā carccitamāṁ niśāmaddhyattil
jagadaṁbā maṭittaṭṭil pūrṇa viśramaṁ
uṇarnnuṇarttē dhyāna navadinaṁ
karma navadinaṁ tyāga sūryaprabhavitaruṁ
prēma navadinaṁ

At night the moonlight bathes the whole world, and Amma's children at the āśraṁ rest in the Cosmic Mother's lap after a hard day's toil. Amma says, "O my darling children, sleep well and be ready in the morning to commence a fresh day contemplating, serving and loving without any expectations."

|| oṁ amṛteśvaryai namaḥ ||

Mēṭam 8, April 21

Praṇāmaṁ

(Prostration)

oṁ kāruṇyākula cittāyai
tyakta-yoga suṣuptaye
keraḷa kṣmāvatīrṇṇāyai
amṛteśvaryai namo namaḥ

O! Pūrṇa-brahma-svarūpiṇī! O Amma! You are an ocean of love and compassion. You, who revel in the highest state of saccidānanda, have come down to us, your children, as our loving mother. Why? Because you want us to become more and more established in the sublime qualities like love, forbearance, compassion, service and charity. To set an example, you embody yourself, again and again as the Mother of the Universe, loving and treating the whole world as your own children.

Amma, I offer my praṇāms at your lotus feet so that I may acquire many of your qualities.

Prabodhanaṁ

(Awakening)

yadā yadāhi dharmasya
glānirbhavati bhārata
abhyutthānaṁ adharmasya
tad-ātmānaṁ sṛjāmyahaṁ
(Bhagavad-Gītā, 4-7)

Amma says:

"My children, why does the supreme truth take birth? God doesn't have to be born because God doesn't need anything from the world. Material wealth and sensual pleasures are meaningless to God. Then what's the importance of a divine incarnation? Seeing the whole world getting deluded by the illusory phenomena of worldly existence, God incarnates to save the entire world from delusion.

"Our Divine Mother comes running with outstretched arms to her children, who are about to sink in the ocean of worldly life. When more and more people become unvirtuous, life in the world becomes intolerable. God incarnates and leads a life of love and service to save the virtuous and to reform the non-virtuous. Spiritual teachers incarnate in succession in Ārṣa Bhāratam [India]. This is the heritage of "the Land of the Sages."

"Look at Śrī Kṛṣṇa, the greatest amongst the ancient teachers. Śrī Kṛṣṇa was a born king. Yet as a child, he played the role of a cowherd and escorted all the cowherd children and their parents in Vṛndāvan and performed all the menial jobs for them. During the Rājasūya Yajña of Yudhiṣṭhīra, Śrī Kṛṣṇa acted as an errand boy for the Pāṇḍavas, maintaining the stores and looking after the needs of all the guests. During the Kurukṣetra War, Śrī Kṛṣṇa played the role of Pārthasārathi, a charioteer, and was also the stable-keeper and so on.

"My children! Learn from Bhagavān Śrī Kṛṣṇa's example. Pray for an expansive heart filled with compassion and eagerness to serve the poor, needy and downtrodden. May you be blessed with the best from the Almighty!"

Prayatnaṁ

(Practice)

The coastal village around Amma's āśraṁ looked very beautiful. The infinite ocean constantly raised the clarion call of Oṁkāra. Līla mōḷ managed to lie down in Saumya's (now Swāminī Kṛṣṇāmṛtā Prāṇā) room on a small coir mat. On entering the room she lifted the mat and found a heap of sand which she cleaned. It was almost like the sandy shore of the sea.

Līla mōḷ's mind was filled with sweet memories of Amma, the infinite ocean of mercy. Līla mōḷ recollects:

Returning after the first visit to Amma, I immediately entered the operation theater. The first patient was a young boy who needed a tonsillectomy. The service of the sick went from 8:00 a.m. to 3:00 p.m. The previous day I had hardly slept. At 3:00 I was about to return to my residence. It was at that time I got a phone call from Dr. Śivarājan, a senior consultant surgeon. A patient with breast cancer was coming in for a radical mastectomy. Although I was feeling very tired, I could not say no. The thought of Amma's omniscience and omnipotence invigorated me. The surgery was supposed to take three hours, but with Amma's grace it finished in a half an hour for Dr. Śivarājan decided it was enough to just remove the tumor and not the entire breast. The patient was awakened from anesthesia, and the doctors were satisfied. It was Amma's wonderful answer to Līla moḷ's prayer for strength: both giving her strength and reducing the length of the surgery. My mind and body felt pervaded with Amma's beautiful presence and power.

Wondering whether Amma has come or not, Līla mōḷ came back to the second night in the āśram.

Pratijñā

(Oath)

This evening I pledge to lead a life of righteousness. Let my life become, from top to bottom, an homage to the supreme truth.

Prārthanā

(Prayer)

praḷayapayōdhijale dhṛtavānasivedaṁ
vihita vahitra caritra makhedaṁ
keśava dhṛtamīnaśarīra
jaya jagadīśa hare, jaya jagadīśa hare
(Aṣṭapadī, 1-1)

When the whole cosmos was dissolved in the cosmic flood, the evil tendencies were hiding the reality of the supreme truth. Then, O my Mother, you incarnated as a big fish and swam to the bottom of the bottomless water and recovered the Vedas.

kannimāsattile kārttikanāḷil
oru gramabhūvilēykkamma vannu
niṅgaḷ ariññīla ñānum arinñīlla
ārārumariyāte amma vannu
kaṅkaḷe mūṭunna bāṣpavarṣaṁ kaiyāl
oppiyeṭukkānāy amma vannu
mūka manassinte tēṅgal kēṭṭīṭuvān
tāmasam-arutē jagad-aṁbikē
tāmasam-arutē jagad-aṁbikē

On the Kārtikā Star of September, Amma came to her coastal village. Without crying she took birth. Amma came to wipe the tears of her children. O Amma! Let there be no delay to remove my sorrow, O Mother of the World.

|| oṁ amṛteśvaryai namaḥ ||

Mēṭam 9, April 22

Praṇāmaṁ

(Prostration)

oṁ mānuṣa strī vapurbhṛte
amṛteśvaryai namo namaḥ
amṛteśvaryai namo namaḥ

Amma! As an ocean of mercy you have taken birth on earth to redeem your children. This time, you have incarnated in the form of the universal mother. You attract your children with your love and actions, thereby enabling them to lead a life of service and righteousness. It is you who show me the correct path and take me to the other shore of life. As your child, I offer my praṇāms at your lotus feet.

Prabodhanaṁ

(Awakening)

ya devi sarva bhūteṣu viṣṇumāyeti śabditā
namastasyai namastasyai namastasyai namo namaḥ
(Devi Māhātmyaṁ)

Amma says:

"My dear sons and daughters, the enlightened sages desire to take birth and lead a life in the world in order to love the Universal Mother. The sages know that the Divine Mother is present in all sentient and nonsentient beings. She alone controls their lives. Sages incarnate to worship the Divine Mother.

"Ordinary folk, hesitate to chant the *Thousand Names of the Divine Mother*, fearing that they may commit errors in pronunciation and thereby invoke her wrath, believing she will curse them.

"When the devotees came to Amma for darśan, Amma had them sit and perform a simple pūjā and also had them chant the holy names of the Divine Mother. Amma was questioned by many who doubted whether her instructions were appropriate.

"Once an arrogant young man was sent by one of the tantrics in northern Kēraḷa to question Amma. Amma and some devotees had just finished chanting the 108 Names of the Divine Mother. As soon as the young man arrived, he asked Amma, "Why did you chant the dhyāna śloka [meditation verse] of the *Lalitā Sahasranāma* (Thousand names of the Divine Mother) and perform the arcana with the 108 Names of Devī?' He was unduly inquisitive, suggesting that the arcana had been performed improperly. Amma replied, 'My son, suppose Amma is speaking English to an audience who does not know the language. Will it do any good? For long, we have created many barriers for the weaker sections of society regarding the worship of God, who is our real self. It is only because Amma is leading the arcana that people come and participate in it.' Then Amma decided to ask him a question in return. She asked him, 'Tell me, who first composed the dhyāna śloka?' He replied, 'It was Lord Śiva.' Amma then said, 'Śiva himself told me that I can do as I like.' The young man was not only dissatisfied but also irritated and he left immediately.

"O my children! Is not the Divine Mother our own mother? Is she not full of compassion and forgiveness? Amma doesn't know Sanskrit or anything, but she knows that our Divine Mother will forgive and forget the mistakes of her ignorant children.

"Suppose a baby that has not yet started speaking properly, calls its father, 'Pa,' will the father be annoyed? On the contrary, he will be delighted and come running to pick up and caress his child. But if the child grows up and then continues to commit the same mistakes, the father might punish him.

"If the temple priests [who perform pūjā as a profession] make a mistake, Amma will not like it. Amma will be angry with them because they call the Divine Mother with a mind full of desires, but that is not the case with innocent or ignorant devotees.

"For instance, consider the fisherman devotee. Jumping into the agitated waters of the river and getting submerged, he cried out, 'Divie Mother! If you don't come just now...' and the Divine Mother rushed to save him. When he was safely out of the water, she blessed him with boons. He said, 'O my Mother, I do not need any boons. Come to my humble abode whenever you feel hungry. I do not have anything great to offer you like temple priests. They make several grand offerings to you and pray to you for delicacies, wealth, power, position, name, fame, wife and children. Will you go to them and bless them?' The Divine Mother agreed, but by then it was noon and the priests had finished the pūjā, taken the prasād (consecrated food offering) and gone away. They were in a hurry to enjoy the sumptuous lunch, so they couldn't receive the Divine Mother's blessings."

Prayatnaṁ

(Practice)

Waiting for Amma and repeating the mantra, "Amma vannō? Amma vannō?" (Has Amma come? Has Amma come?) until midnight, Līla mōḷ finally heard that Amma had come. She got up and ran. The stars were smiling in the sky. Below, on earth, the leaves were dancing, and the birds were singing. She sat down after prostrating at Amma's sacred feet. Amma told her, "My daughter has been here since noon. Someone could have brought you to Kollam. I was looking for you the whole day. Tomorrow Amma will talk to you. My daughter, now go and sleep."

Amma was sitting under the ñāval tree. The branches of the sprawling tree were embracing the earth. Under the tree, was Mātā Amṛrtānandamayī Devī, the all-pervading tree, giving shade to the whole world. Amma shades all children from scorching heat of worldly existence.

One devotee, Sarasamma from Karunāgappaḷḷi had come with Amma. She said to Amma, "Amma! It is only due to your blessings that my asthma does not bother me nowadays."

Amma asked her, "Do you continue to take the Tuesday mauna vrata and upāsana [vow of silence and worship]." She said, "Amma, how can I stop it? How can we forget that it is Amma who gave back my husband's lost job and our house? Amma, it is you who provide us with our daily food."

Amma's would laugh and tease her and give her a soft, loving push. Pointing to Līla Mōḷ, her new daughter, Amma asked Sārasamma, "Don't you see that my darling daughter has come?" and she lovingly coaxed her to sleep. Yet her daughter managed to sit there for a while before retiring to the room where she was to relax. It was not to sleep but to awaken to the eternal real existence. It was not to languish in ignorance, but to bask in the bliss of direct experience of absolute knowledge that is Amma.

Pratijñā

(Oath)

From material treasures to eternal values. From selfish interest to broadminded service. From the narrow circle of family life to seeking of God and attaining the Supreme.

Prārthanā

(Prayer)

na guroradhikaṁ tattvaṁ
na guroradhikaṁ tapaḥ
tatva jñānād-paraṁ nāsti
tasmai śrī gurave namaḥ
(Guru Gītā)

Nothing exists beyond the guru, and there is no greater austerity than living with the guru. The greatest knowledge is the knowledge that the guru awakens in the disciple. To such a guru, I bow down and pray for the guru's grace.

orōrō vidyakaḷ ōti paṭikkēṇṭa
tānē udikkuṁ manasu tannil
pārāte tōnnuṁ atinuḷḷōr artthavuṁ
nityaṁ gurū pādaṁ kumbiṭunnēn
avvannumuḷḷa guru bhakti eṅkilō
ī vaṇṇaṁ mattāruṁ illennākuṁ
vevvēre vannīṭuṁ bhaktiyuṁ muktiyuṁ
nityaṁ guru pādaṁ kumbiṭunnēn

One doesn't have to acquire all branches of knowledge; all knowledge together with the inner meanings automatically awakens in one's heart. I therefore bow down always at the sacred feet of the guru, who accomplishes this task.

One who has real devotion to one's guru will attain the ultimate. Devotion and liberation will come to him or her in full measure. I bow down at the sacred feet of the guru, who makes this possible.

|| oṁ amṛteśvaryai namaḥ ||

Mēṭam 10, April 23

Praṇāmaṁ

(Prostration)

oṁ mātā pitṛ cirā cīrṇa puṇya pura phalātmane
amṛteśvaryai namo namaḥ
amṛteśvaryai namo namaḥ

Let me offer my prostrations at your holy feet, this divine morning. God who is beyond birth and death has incarnated in this age in your form. You have for a long time performed several holy rituals and engaged yourself in various activities in the family, in society and in the world at large. You were born to your parents as a divine daughter and then you reached the status of the Holy Mother of the Universe. O Amma! Bless your children and let me bow down again and again to you.

Prabodhanaṁ

(Awakening)

svāmin namaste nata lōka bandho
kāruṇya sindho patitaṁ bhavābdhau
mām-uddhara ātmīya kaṭākṣa dṛṣṭyā
ṛjvādi kāruṇya sudhābhi vṛṣṭyā
(Vivēkacūḍāmaṇi)

Amma says:

"My children, the disciple who has reached his guru, submits himself to him with the following words full of bliss:

"'Swāmī! I surrender to you my self-centered life, which is full of sorrows. You are the sole refuge of those who are humble. You are an ocean of mercy. I have fallen in the ocean of this worldly life. Kindly lift me up, my lord. Look after me kindly, showering amṛta—the nectar of immortality.'

"'Swāmī! You have been my master in my previous births, and you will continue to be my master in all my future births. Kindly accept my humble praṇāms to you. It is you who can save me from the cycle of birth and death.'

"This is the right prayer of a fit disciple. There is another category of disciples. Observing the guru, he thought, 'What is this? He seems to be an ordinary human being, but he is being worshiped by others and is also given a high status and wealth. Let me observe what is happening here. If only I could be like him!' He approached the man who was called a guru and praised him, 'O Guru! How great you are! Please accept me as your servant.' The guru agreed and asked him, 'What will you do here? Don't you know that service is the most difficult task?'

"'Gurudeva, I am ready to do anything you ask me to do.'

"'You have to get up during the brahma muhūrta.'

"'What is that muhūrta?'

"'I shall tell you. It is the time between 3:00 and 6:00 in the morning. Our intellect will be inspired during this very holy time. The brahmacārīs and others in the three āśramas must be up and doing their sādhanā at this time.'

"'Guruji! I do not understand. Who is a brahmacārī? What are the three āśramas? Are there two more āśramas here?'

"Laughing, the guru said, 'You are my best disciple. You have a mind to ask and understand. My son, a brahmacārī is the one who stays with the guru day and night for spiritual education.'

"'Oh, now I understand. But where are the other āśramas?'

"'The three āśramas are the different ghaṭṭas, or stages of life.'

"'What are these ghattạs? I have heard of pūrva and paściṁ ghaṭṭams.'

"With a hint of sarcasm, the guru said, 'My dear one, what you say is correct! These gatas are different stages of our life. After one's education is complete, one becomes established in the knowledge of the Vedas, Vedāṅgas, itihāsas and purāṇas. To practice this knowledge in life is the next gata, meaning the householder's life. The guru gives the farewell words of blessing as he returns home.'

"'What are the words of blessings of the guru?'

"'My son, in course of time, you will learn everything.'

"The disciple lost patience. He thought he would leave the place soon and said, 'My Guru, your words sounded sweet to me. I feel that I must be a guru and not a disciple.'

"See, my darling children, most of the disciples of this age are of this type. Amma is not telling you this story to make you frustrated but to make you more cautious. You must be always active and advancing. Amma is with you."

Prayatnaṁ

(Practice)

That night, Līla mōḷ returned to Brahmacāriṇī Saumya's room, as Amma had asked her to do so. Amma was still sitting under the tree. The true being of this daughter was with Amma. It was as if only the body was lying on the mat spread in the room.

The ocean, which is the eternal resounder of oṁkāra, was just outside the āśram. Viśvamātā, the Universal Mother, who is an oṁkāra va, the personification of Oṁ, was in the āśram in the small frame of her human body under the ñāval tree. Amma appeared to her to be the personification of discrimination and dispassion. Amma was immersed in total bliss under the sky studded with glittering stars.

Amma does not desire anything nor is there anything that she cannot acquire. Never is she touched by sorrows! Never is she inactive! Incessantly, she works for the world at large. Amma just prays, jokes, laughs and talks with all who come to her and acts like an innocent girl who does not know anything of the world. Is there any end to this ocean of compassion?

Līla mōḷ recollects:

Today, I was about to fall into a difficult situation. It was Amma's grace that saved me. In the morning, I was about to acquire the priority coupon in the government bus stand at Tiruvanantapuram. I happened to mention the place of my destination incorrectly. Instead of Karunāgappaḷḷi, I said Kaññirappaḷḷi, which is very far away in the high ranges. Suddenly, as if prompted by someone internally I said, "Ōccīra," and it was possible for me to reach the āśram.

In the āśram at noon, Amma's father, having heard about this, advised me, "Hereafter, my daughter, do not get down at Ōccīra. Come through Karunāgappaḷḷi. Ōccīra is not a reliable place for you."

Pratijñā

(Oath)

In the journey of life, I will take care not to follow the wrong path. I shall advance on the right path. Praying to Amma, I shall always strive to reach the supreme goal.

Prārthanā

(Prayer)

namo devyai mahā devyai śivāyai satataṁ namaḥ
namaḥ prakṛtyai bhadrāyai niyatāḥ praṇatāḥ smatāṁ
(Dēvī Māhātmyaṁ)

Bowing down to the self-effulgent Bhagavatī! Bowing down to the Devī who is worshiped by the great Brahmā, Viṣṇu and Maheśvara! Bowing down to the Divine Mother who is the sole protector! Bowing down to the Divine Mother who is the cause of this world. Bowing down to the Divine Mother who bestows the auspicious fruit of all the karmas. We offer our humble prayers to the Divine Mother, prostrating at her divine feet. The import of the great word "namaḥ" is the yearning to become identified with the object of prostration. Here, the jīva wants to be one with Śiva.

Amma, to perceive this truth, bless your children with strength and devotion today!

kaṇṇanuṁ ammayuṁ onnāṇō
cid-ākāśa sīmayil annoru ghanaśyāma mēghaṁ
varaṇṭa vāṭikayil viṇṭuṁ vasantaṁ pōl-amma
kaṇṇanāyi vannu kaṇṇanāyi vannu
jīvita nabhō vīthiyil mārivil prabhāpūraṁ
iruṇṭa cakra vāḷattil udaya sūryan pōlamma

dēvi ammayāyi dēvi ammayāyi
sūrya-prabahayil mazhavil varnnaṅgalpol
ammayil rūpa vaividhyaṁ

Are Amma and Śrī Kṛṣṇa one and the same?
In the boundless horizon of cid-ākāśa—the expanse
of consciousness—is the ghanaśyāma mēghaṁ—
the dense blue cloud that is Śrī Kṛṣṇa.
In the withered garden, returns the spring that is
Amma, the Divine Mother as Śrī Kṛṣṇa.
In the horizon of life, there appears the
rainbow of colors, full of radiance.
In the dark horizon, there appears the rising
sun that is the Divine Mother.
In the rays of the sun are seven different shades.
Likewise, in Amma's luminous form are numerous forms.
Amma, to perceive this truth, bless your children
with strength and devotion today!

|| oṁ amṛteśvaryai namaḥ ||

Mēṭam 11 April 24

Praṇāmaṁ

(Prostration)

Oṁ niśabda jananī garbha nirgamātbhuta karmaṇe
amṛteśvaryai namo namaḥ
amṛteśvaryai namo namaḥ

Amma! You have, in truth, no birth or death. How amazing! You did not cry when you were born on earth. Amma, my whole life is verily a constant crying. I beg of you, bless me with the eternal beatitude and knowledge of the Absolute, and I prostrate at your lotus feet.

Prabodhanaṁ

(Awakening)

bahūnāmemi prathamo
bahūnāmemi maddhyamaḥ
kiṁ svid yamsya karttavyaṁ
yanmayādya kariṣyati
(Kaṭhopaniṣad, 1-1-5)

Amma says:

"My dear children, in this world, we can see all sorts of students and children. You should aspire to be an ideal child of your parents. How can you accomplish this objective? Amma would like to tell you a story from the great epic, the *Rāmāyaṇa*.

"King Daśāratha wanted to crown his eldest and dearest son, Śrī Rāma as king of Ayodhyā. All the necessary arrangements for the coronation ceremony were being made. But the evil-minded Mantharā [maid to the second-queen Kaikeyī] convinced Kaikeyī to call upon the boons bestowed upon her by the king for saving his life. She asked for her own son Bhārata to be crowned king and Śrī Rāma to be sent into exile.

"King Daśāratha was grief-stricken and almost on the verge of losing his life. Yet he wished to keep his word to his queen Kaikeyī. Śrī Rāma was called immediately to the palace. King Daśāratha was so upset that he could not even divulge the reason for his acute sorrow. In a trembling voice he could only utter, 'O Rāma, O Rāma.' Śrī Rāma promised the king that he would fulfill his father's wish, whatever it be. Of course, Śrī Rāma was an ideal son and supremely virtuous.

"See, my children, those who perform their duties towards their parents without even being asked to do so are ideal children and are regarded as supreme. Those who carry out their parents' wishes when they are requested to do so can be considered to be mediocre, while those who fail to do their duties even when they are reminded of it, are inferior.

"Look at Nāciketas, the little child of Kaṭhopaniṣad. He was so brave that he was able to remind his father of his duty while he was performing the great sacrifice. The father of Nāciketas, who was the king, was supposed to donate all that he possessed at the end of a sacrificial ceremony. The king pondered over the fate of his son if he gave away everything in charity and so he presented the Brahmins with old cows that were incapable of yielding milk or begetting calves.

"You may wonder about the importance of cows and calves? In olden times, cows were considered as the greatest wealth. Amma wants her children to be discriminating and understand that, of late, people have begun to underestimate the utility of cows and bullocks and are becoming really foolish. People stoop so slow as to extract every drop of milk from the cows and then sell the poor animal to the butchers. Even tender calves are killed and eaten."

Prayatnaṁ

(Practice)

It was 10:00 in the morning. Amma was giving darśan in the balcony of the small temple and talking to a small group of devotees. Līla mōḷ, who had arrived the previous day, was sitting among the devotees and observing Amma closely. Amma was smiling at everyone and speaking. Amma sang "Ellareyuṁ koṇṭupona śivanē ennekuṭe koṇṭupoṭa śivane." (Lord Śiva, you are the one who absorbs everyone unto yourself forever. Why are you leaving me behind? Kindly take me also with you.)

At that time this daughter was thinking, "Amma told me last night that she would talk to me in private. Now, Amma is not even looking at me. I will have to go back to my former place—is that the meaning of this silence? How long should I wait? Yes, Amma told me during my last visit that I should take two or three days leave and come back. Now, Amma's words have come true."

I had kept my resignation letter for Swāmiji's (the hospital president of the Rāmakṛṣṇa Āśram Hospital) approval in the office and had also written a personal letter. That was why I was so anxious to hear words of Amma's approval of my coming and joining the āśram.

While my thoughts were flowing in this direction, Amma was laughing loudly. She called little Śivan [Amma's nephew] and made him sit on her lap. She made Śivan sit in padmāsanam [lotus-pose] with his hands in cinmudrā. Amma jokingly told him "Śiva, you can have apples and grapes if you like, but you first must meditate some." No sooner did Śivan hear this than he sat in meditation. Amma chanted Oṁ three times and Śivan responded. After a little while, he opened his eyes and began eating the fruits, which Amma had kept in front of him.

Amma asked Śivan, "Do you remember the guru-disciple story? Tell us now." Śivan kept quiet. Then Amma started the story:

"A guru and his disciples were traveling in a bullock cart. Purposely, the guru, in order to test his disciples, told them, 'I am going to rest for a while. My children, you must look after my belongings.'

"The disciples readily agreed. One by one, all the guru's luggage fell out of the cart, and the disciples simply gazed at them and sat unmoved. When the guru opened his eyes and looked for his things, he could not find anything. He enquired, 'My sons, where are my things?'

"They informed him that things had fallen down on the road. The guru asked them why they had not put the things back in the cart. They stated that they were just obeying his instructions and said, 'Don't you remember that you instructed us to keep on looking at them? We did that.'

"The guru said, 'Oh, my foolish disciples, hereafter, don't miss anything. You must put back in the cart whatever fall out.'

"The disciples agreed. They proceeded with the journey. As he rested, the guru was becoming increasingly aware of the odor of cow dung. He wanted to know what was happening. One of the disciples said, 'O my revered teacher, this time we have obeyed your words. You had told us to put back in the cart whatever was falling out, so when the bullocks were excreting, we picked up the dung and put it in the cart.'

"The guru said, 'Oh! Now I have come to my senses. Now I will have to give you a list of things.' The guru made a list of items and gave it to the senior disciple and told him, 'I trust you; don't let me down,' and he kept aloof.

"While traveling, the cart hit a small ditch. The guru happened to bounce out of the cart. The foolish disciples kept on driving the cart as if nothing had happened. The guru shouted, 'Stop! Stop!' Finally, they stopped the cart and approached the guru, who asked them, 'Why didn't you take care of me when I fell out of the cart?'

"The disciples answered, 'We went through the list that you had given us and we never found your name on it.'

Līla mōḷ wanted to laugh. The story summed up her own mental state. She thought, "Amma was telling the story for my sake. Why should I be anxious when I have a guru who responds to each and every one of my thoughts?"

Pratijñā

(Oath)

I will constantly contemplate upon Amma's
invaluable teachings and attempt to live accordingly
so as to become Amma's darling child.

Prārthanā

(Prayer)

akhaṇdha maṇḍalākāraṁ
vyāptaṁ yena carācaraṁ

tat padaṁ darśitaṁ yena
tasmai śrī gurave namaḥ
(Guru Gītā)

I pray to you, the absolute indivisible consciousness,
who is our sole protector and teacher.

ammē jaga jananī
nāḷituvareyuṁ nīyenikkanyayāy
ajñātayāy nāmamātrayāy
eṅgō ni vasiccu
ammē mama jananī
muḷkkāṭṭil oru nalla pūmoṭṭupōl
iruṇṭa vīthiyil oḷināḷaṁpōl
niśayile nīlatārakapōle
taḷarnna tāmara malarāṁ manassin savitāvāy
piṭayuṁ prāṇanu punarujīvaniyāy
uḷḷiloruparaṁ poruḷāy
udayaṁ ceytu nin kuññinabhayamēki
ammē priya jananī ammē priya jananī

O Mother of the Universe, all these days you have been away from me almost unknown to me, known only by name, O my Mother. You are like a blossom among the dense thorny bush; a flame on the dark path; a glittering star of the dark night; a sun for the closed lotus of the mind; life force for this collapsing child of yours; and o supreme life! you have awakened inspiration in me and you have made me your own. O Dearest Mother! O Dearest Mother!

|| oṁ amṛteśvaryai namaḥ ||

Mēṭam 12, April 25

Praṇāmaṁ

(Prostration)

oṁ kāḷī śrī kṛṣṇa sankāśa kōmaḷa śyāmaḷa tviṣe
amṛteśvaryai namo namaḥ
amṛteśvaryai namo namaḥ

Amma! O Kāḷī, Kṛṣṇa Rūpiṇi! You, who were born as a dark-colored sweet baby, attract one and all by your enchanting smile. To you, I offer my praṇāms, praying for a happy day.

Prabodhanaṁ

(Awakening)

satyaṁ brūyāt priyaṁ brūyāt
na brūyāt satyaṁ apriyam
[Subhāṣitam]

Amma says:

"My darling children! In the ocean of our scriptures is hidden countless, priceless pearls and invaluable gems. In a syllable, a word, or in a sentence, the whole import of the scriptural message has been conveyed. This is the unique style of Vedānta.

"Once the devas, asuras and humans approached their great father, Lord Brahmā, in order to learn. So, father Brahmā assigned a project of engaging in the austerities of a student's life for several years. All three groups of his children readily completed the study and returned. Now they wanted to receive the concluding instructions.

"The creator, Brahmā, looked at his darling children and uttered the syllable 'da.' Then the devas asked Him, 'O dear, great Father! You mean dāmyata [to have self-control]?' Brahmā agreed.

Then the humans asked Brahmā, 'Of course, you meant 'datta' [to be charitable]?' He agreed. Then the asuras asked him, 'Is not dayadhvam [to be compassionate], the meaning of da?' He agreed again.

"Lord Brahmā was very glad that his students understood him. They went back to their usual lives, performed their duties according to the instructions that they had received and attained victory. The whole world resounded 'da... da... da...' with the clouds.

"This thunder of 'da... da... da...' will awaken my children, Amma hopes. You will have dama [self-control], dānam [charity] and dayā [compassion]. Any unpleasant truth should be spoken by you in a pleasant way.

"Suppose one was born with squinty eyes. Isn't it rude to call him 'Squinty'? If you do that, his life will become an intolerable hell. A volcano of resentment will form within him and eventually erupt, and we will be responsible.

"Amma shall illustrate this with a small story. Once, a father, mother and their only son were expecting a guest who had an unusually large nose. The little son was very innocent. Therefore, the parents instructed him, 'Please be careful and refrain from commenting on our guest's nose.' The son readily agreed. The guest arrived for dinner. While they were having dinner, the son was so amazed to see the huge nose of the guest that he forgot to eat. Seeing their son, the parents were feeling agitated. They communicated to their son using signs. The son pointed at the guest's nose and responded, 'No, No, I am not saying anything. I'm just looking at it.' Amma does not have to tell you how the guest must have felt.

"It is our tongue that is our friend and foe. Once there was a dispute between the teeth and the tongue. The 32 teeth, in unison, told the tongue, 'You are enjoying food. We are doing the work of chewing. This is not fair.' They threatened the tongue, 'If we bite you, all your privileges will vanish. Beware! We are 32 in number and you are alone.' The tongue replied, 'You are right. But don't you know that if I utter a word against someone and annoy him, he will knock you all out?' Hearing this, the teeth came to their senses and kept quiet.

"What have you learned from this story? The tongue, which is very difficult to control, must be trained to speak properly, otherwise the harm is not for the teeth alone but for all that belongs to you.

"My children, you must talk only when it is necessary. Amma prescribes a day of maunam [silence] once a week and a restricted diet. This is very much needed during bad times. My children! Do not wait for the bad times to begin. Begin your austerities now."

Prayatnaṁ

(Practice)

In the kaḷari [little temple], Līla mōḷ was sitting, savoring the nectar of Amma's words. She was very happy. Amma went on speaking to the devotees and was ignoring her daughter. Yet Līla mōḷ's mind was calm and strong and she could wait until Amma chose to talk to her. She could realize that this was Amma's test in order to make her understand that the path of seeking God is as sharp as the razor's edge. After a while, Amma got up and returned to her room. And this daughter returned to her own world of spiritual unrest.

The āśramites and the devotees who were present were engaged in the work of publishing the āśram magazine. When the bhajans were over, Amma would also join them. The daughter remembered the day when she received the magazine by post.

Līla mōḷ recollects:

I was waiting for Amma with tears in my eyes. One day the postman delivered a letter and a magazine. The letter read: "It was when I happened to be in the Mātā Amṛitānandamayi Math that I came to know that the magazine *Amṛtavāhini* had already been released. I remembered you and gave your address. Amma was very happy about it. I have paid the subscription. If you feel inclined, you may donate some amount to the āśram."

I felt that what had happened was very auspicious. It appeared as if the magazine was a messenger of Amma. Until then, I did not know how to communicate with Amma and the āśram. Now I could write a letter in reply and apply for a subscription.

Subsequently, life went on as usual with my work at the hospital. It was then that I became the owner of an invaluable treasure–Amma's letter. On the envelope, there was the emblem and address of the Mātā Amṛtānandamayī Maṭh. With trembling hands, I opened the letter and started reading.

Amma had written:

"My darling daughter, you are engaged in service-oriented work. That is very good. Amma knows that there is no one to assist you and sometimes you become weak and exhausted. If you chant your mantra, you will be protected. Dear daughter! Amma will write more later. Daughter, Amma's loving kisses."

It was very difficult to read Amma's letter because of tears filling the eyes.

While reading Amma's letter that day, I was convinced that if we put forth a little effort or took a small step towards Amma, Amma would take a hundred steps towards us.

The letter from Amma–who is by no means an ordinary teacher–and the prospect of having her darśan soon gave me joy beyond words. While absorbed in thoughts of Amma's motherly love, this daughter heard someone calling out and saying, "Amma is going to the seashore and she wants you to follow her."

Pratijñā

(Oath)

If we take a step towards Amma, Amma will take a hundred steps towards us. What a Divine Mother! I will follow her and I will never forget her. My life will be an incessant effort to hold on to her.

Prārthanā

(Prayer)

hiraṇmayena pātreṇa
satyasyāpihitaṁ mukhaṁ
tattvaṁ pūṣaṇṇapāvṛṇū
satya dharmāya dṛṣtaye
(Īśāvāsya Upaniṣad, 15)

O Sūrya Deva! The face of truth is veiled by a golden covering. You are the one who is omniscient and omnipotent. Kindly remove the veil to enable me to perceive truth and dharma.

kaṇṇanuṁ ammayuṁ onnāṇō? atumituvum eṅgane onnākuṁ?
sūryaprabhayil mazhavil varṇṇaṅgaḷpōl ammayil rūpa vaividhyaṁ
ā ī dēvadattan ennuḷḷoru collil raṇṭumorē dēvadattan
kaṇṇanōṭamma karayunnu pāṭunnu vēre vēre ennu tōnnuṁ
makkaḷkku mātṛka kāṭṭikkoṭuttiṭ duhkha nivṛtti varuttān
kaṇṇā ni enne marannuvōyennamma pāṭuṁ cilappōḷ karayuṁ
makkaḷkku mārga nirdēśavuṁ jīvita lakṣya subhōdhavuṁ nalkān
bhaṣaṇaṁ īvidhaṁ kēṭṭappōḷ bhaktaykk saṁśayaṁ tīrukayāyi
satyānubhavavuṁ annutannē amma nalki anugrahiccallō
darśana bhajanayil annutanne amma kannaniyennu pāṭumbol
onnil anēkavuṁ, anēkattil onnumāy mālayil nūlupōl amma
ennile saṁśayaṁ niṅguvān kākkaṇe ennenuṁ uḷḷil viḷaṅgīṭaṇē

One devotee asks, "Are Amma and Śrī Kṛṣṇa one? How can that and this be one?"

I explain: "As in the sun rays, the seven colors of the rainbow are intrinsic, so also in Amma, the different forms are immanent. As illustrated in the Vedāntic words, 'This and that Devadatta are the one and the same.'"

Amma sings and cries to Śrī Kṛṣṇa, as though she, like Mīrabai, is but an ardent devotee of Kṛṣṇa—though she is in essence Śrī Kṛṣṇa himself in a different form. This is to set an example and remove the mental distractions and frustrations of her children. For instance, Amma sings, "Kaṇṇā ni enne marannuvō?" (Have you forgotten me, dear Kṛṣṇa?) and sheds tears in order to demonstrate to her children how to cry to God, making the effort to reach God easier."

Hearing this, the devotee is cleared of his doubts. Moreover, the devotee could directly experience Amma's divinity and love for her children when unexpectedly and unusually she sang "Kaṇṇā ni enne marannuvō?" the same day. It was during the pre-bhāva darśan bhajans, which started by 5:00 in the evening.

The unity underlying this diversity is like the thread in a garland of flowers. O Amma, be kind enough to come into my heart and remove all my doubts.

|| oṁ amṛteśvaryai namaḥ ||

Mēṭam 13, April 26

Praṇāmaṁ

(Prostration)

oṁ ciranaṣṭa punarlabdha bhārgava kṣetra sampade
amṛteśvaryai namo namaḥ
amṛteśvaryai namo namaḥ

Amma! You are the personification of love and compassion. This land of the Great Sage Paraśurāma was becoming increasingly enmeshed in the darkness of ignorance. That is the reason you incarnated in Kēraḷa to alleviate suffering of your children, by showing them the correct way of living. Let me offer my most humble praṇāms at your lotus feet. Kindly save me.

Prabodhanaṁ

(Awakening)

satyameva jayate nā anṛtaṁ
(Muṇḍaka Upaniṣad, 1-6)

Amma says:

"O my children! God is truth. You can know God by adhering to truth. When the sun rises, there is no more darkness. Likewise, when the God of truth and love comes to us, untruth and hatred will cease to exist. The festivity of equality and godliness will prevail.

"You are all familiar with the Ōṇaṁ song that goes: māvēli nāṭu vāṇīṭuṁ kālaṁ. It is told that during the reign of King Mahābali, no one lied and cheated and no untruthful words were uttered. Can you tell me the reason? Yes, yes, you are right. King Mahābali was a great devotee of Lord Mahāviṣṇu. King Mahābali even went against his guru's instruction and promised to donate whatever his divine guest demanded. Mahāviṣṇu, who came in the form of a Vāmana—a dwarfish brahmacārī, asked the great king for a little piece of land, measuring an area covered by his three footsteps. King Mahābali acceded to his request. Mahāviṣṇu immediately expanded his diminutive form and measured the entire cosmos in two steps. As there was no space left for the Lord to take his third footstep, King Mahābali offered his own head for the Lord to place his foot on, thereby surrendering himself to the Lord.

"Bhagavān himself, during Rāma Āvatara, abandoned his kingdom and went away to lead a life in the forest. That is why Śrī Rāma is said to be an incarnation of dharma. Dharma is the way of life that sustains the world and enables the world to hold on to truth, charity, mercy and perseverance. In Kaliyugam, dharma is said to have only one foot, representing truth. What happened to the other three feet represented by charity, compassion and control of the senses and mind? One by one they were amputated, in the course of Kṛtayugam, Tretāyugam and Dvāparayugm. My children, you may wonder what you should do! Try your utmost to lead a truthful life. Amma is very particular about this. All the great ones of the past have set examples of a truthful life. The great King Hariścandra had to undergo many difficult tests before he finally succeeded. Let us look at the more recent examples. Amma means the example of Gāndhiji who by living a life of truth and love inspired many of his comrades to fight for freedom and finally won svarāj [independence] for India. As a great devotee poet put it, 'We, who are born as human beings in the land of Bhārat, must not at any cost forsake truth and dharma.'"

Prayatnaṁ

(Practice)

Līla mōḷ recollects:

The consent given by Amma, though not in words, through the guru-disciple story was consoling to Līla mōḷ. Her heart was full of the blissful thoughts of becoming an āśramite, for which Amma had given her silent consent. In the evening Amma was going to the seashore along with a few of the āśramites and devotees and Līla mōḷ could also follow Amma. It was her long-cherished wish to meditate on the seashore with Amma and her wish was going to be fulfilled. Amma and the devotees were walking through a narrow pathway in front of the āśram towards the seashore and Līla mōḷ joined them. Amma, who is always benevolent to the devotees, was supporting one of her most senior devotees, Śrī Ōṭṭur Unninaṁbūritippāṭ. His nephew was also in the group. Ōṭṭūr, a great scholar and poet and a devout seeker, was having a childlike attitude towards Amma and he was putting forward many questions to Amma.

Amma was answering all his queries in her own unique way, and this special devotee was very pleased. Amma used to call him "O my darling Unni Kaṇṇan mōn" [little Kṛṣṇa son]. She enjoyed his childlike behavior, and she would express it by her usual sweet smile and affection.

As soon as Amma reached the seashore, she sat down with her disciples on the sand. When Amma loudly chanted Oṁ, all responded to it and made an earnest effort to concentrate on the divine syllable. Soon everyone appeared to be meditating, and it started raining, though all were indifferent to the big rain drops. Līla mōḷ thought for a moment, "I am prone to catch cold and cough very easily. Maybe it is the effect of the anesthetic gases in the operating theater. Should I get up?" She didn't make any conscious response to this thought. Amma was sitting like a rock, without any movement. Līla mōḷ was most impressed by Amma's equanimity to rain or shine. She made up her mind to go deeper into meditation by thinking of Amma.

After a while, the rain stopped. Amma was returning to the āśram. While passing by, Amma stopped near Līla mōḷ, who was still sitting. Līla mōḷ suddenly got up and followed Amma. Her mind was still and blissful. This bliss which she enjoyed gave her a glimpse of the truth, which is beyond dualities like happiness and misery, heat and cold, etc. She also realized that this eternal happiness, which is most subtle and which has no beginning or end, is now, as if personified in the form of Amma.

Pratijñā

(Oath)

Day by day I shall strive to imbibe the teachings
of the guru and live accordingly.

Prārthanā

(Prayer)

brahmānandaṁ paramasukhadaṁ kēvalaṁ jñānamūrtiṁ
dvandātītaṁ gaganasadṛśaṁ tatvamasyādi lakṣyaṁ
ēkaṁ nityaṁ vimalamacalaṁ sarvadhī sākṣibhūtaṁ
bhāvātītaṁ triguṇarahitaṁ sad-guruṁ taṁ namāmi
(Guru Gītā)

O Amma, the personification of eternal happiness,
who is beyond the dualities of happiness and
misery, kindly shine in my heart.

āyiraṁ kōṭi sūryaprabhāpūrṇṇayāy

hṛttilennamma vannettumeṅkil
satyattin ponprabha eṅguṁ parattunna
sundara suprabhātaṁ viṭaruṁ

O Amma, if you come to my heart with your effulgence
of thousands of suns, then will the morning of
the golden light of truth dawn in my life.

|| oṁ amṛteśvaryai namaḥ ||

Mēṭam 14, April 27

Praṇāmaṁ

(Prostration)

oṁ mṛta prāya bhṛgu kṣētra punaruddhita tejase
amṛteśvaryai namo namaḥ
amṛteśvaryai namo namaḥ

The great Paraśurāma reclaimed this land of Kēraḷa and erected a beautiful shrine of eternal values. In course of time, the daily worship in this shrine ceased and the whole country verged on collapse. It was then that Amma personified herself to establish the worship of good qualities and started rejuvenating the whole world, starting from her own place of birth. O Amma! You are the protector of all the eternal values and I, your child, again and again offer my praṇāms to you.

Prabodhanaṁ

(Awakening)

namaḥ pada samarppaṇād
aparamastikiṁ tarppaṇaṁ
(Subhāṣitaṁ)

Amma says:

"My children, all of you are familiar with the word namaḥ. Have you contemplated the meaning of this word? You must be conscious of the greatness of this word; only then can you chant your prayers and mantras properly. Every namaḥ is of great importance. But if you chant it without devotion and śraddha [concentration], you may not get the real benefit. God forgives the mistakes of his ignorant children, but if the necessary effort is not made to correct yourself and strengthen love and devotion, mere mechanical chanting of mantras won't do any good.

"The implied meaning of the word namaḥ is 'na mama' [not mine, but yours]. We pray to God to bless us with sincerity so that we may become conscious of the fact that everything in this world belongs to God alone and not us. With this attitude, if you repeat the prayers and the mantras, all your problems in life will be solved in due course.

"Suppose you are taking a boat to cross the backwater. You may carry your luggage in your hand all the way, but once you are in the boat you can set your luggage down. Similarly, once you surrender to God, you can leave all your burdens to God. Once we are merged with God, as a drop of water with the ocean, we acquire the strength of God. When we surrender our small 'I' to the great cosmic ego, we become one with the Totality. We acquire the qualities of God, who is omnipotent, omniscient and omnipresent. The importance of the word namaḥ reminds us of the importance of self-surrender. Usually, the repetition of a word is boring to us but that is not the case with this unique word, namaḥ. In mantras and hymns, we can see this word very often repeated. To minimize the wandering of the mind, and to reduce the number of evil thoughts, this word is of great use.

"Why should a human being bow down to another one? Amma shall narrate a story: Once a young Westerner came to our āśram. He was addicted to smoking ganja. He sat and started smoking, right in the front yard of the āśram. The āśramites told him, 'What you are doing is against the āśraṁ rules and the law. You cannot stay here anymore.'

"Hearing this, the young man got very upset. He shouted, 'Don't you know that I am not subject to your rules and regulations? I am my own boss.' He did not even move from his seat. Regardless, he soon left. On his way to Kollaṁ, he was arrested and kept in police custody. There, he was treated like a prisoner. He had no freedom whatsoever. He could no longer do as he liked. As soon as he was released from the prison, he came back to the āśram. This time, he was a changed person. He told the brahmacārīs, 'You were right. Now I know that I am not my own boss.'"

Prayatnaṁ

(Practice)

The experiences which Līla mōḷ had while she was in the company of Amma had made her patient enough to wait for Amma's instructions regarding her permanent stay in the āśram. She had to be absolutely obedient to Amma. She was waiting to receive Amma's call. But she was not called by Amma on the second day of her arrival also. "Now, two days have gone by," she thought.

Līla mōḷ recollects:

Yesterday, after having returned from the seashore we could sit with Amma while she was singing the evening bhajans. How long I had waited for this moment. Fortunately, I had the opportunity to read the songs that Śrī Rāmakṛṣṇa used to sing from the book *The Gospel of Rāmakṛṣṇa*.' I cannot express the sweetness of the songs in words. I have a mental picture of Śrī Bhagavān singing the bhajans with his young disciples Narendra [Swāmī Vivekānanda] and the rest. How lucky I am to see Amma singing and listen to the sweet melodies. Although I was not a good singer, I yearned to sing during the bhāva darśan.

Almost the whole night would be spent in bhajanānanda and brahmānanda–the bliss of worship and the Self. Everyone around would be immersed in bliss.

Once a swāmiji came to Rāmakṛṣṇa Math Hospital where I was working. He told me that he had been to Amma's āśram, and he showed me the pamphlet that he had printed. It was very well printed with Amma's photos in Kṛṣṇa Bhāva and Devi Bhāva together with various pictures of the āśram. What a real treat it was! I cannot explain what sort of change came over my mind when I saw Amma standing in Kṛṣṇa Bhāva. A sea of spiritual emotions surged through me. Radiant eyes of Kaṇṇa, so penetrating, soul-stirring, were the source of this sea of emotions. I was suddenly immersed in a sea of love.

The swāmiji told me that while Amma was giving darśan at night, in this divine mood, the villagers flocked around her with their little worries and problems. Amma would come to them and accept all their problems as her own. They would be relieved of their mental tension and when they returned home they would find that Amma had removed all obstacles from the path of their lives. Food, clothing and shelter were the main things they wanted to have and all these were found to have been provided. I felt that what he said was all so familiar to me and that I was going to witness everything with my own eyes. Right in front of me, I would be able to perceive Amma's divine beauty during Kṛṣṇa Bhāva, the dark blue hue of Kṛṣṇa, radiating all around and sending the thronging devotees into rapture.

The continuity of this daughter's thoughts was broken for the time being. The āśramites were busy arranging for the Bhāva Darśan. She remembered Amma telling her about the importance of sitting and meditating in the little temple while Amma's bhāva darśan was going on.

Pratijñā

(Oath)

From the limitations and conditioning of the body,
I shall try to release the mind and raise it to the
infinite expanse of the absolute reality. Selfishness
will be replaced by concern for the whole world.

Prārthanā

(Prayer)

śaraṇāgata dīnārta paritrāṇa parāyaṇe
sarvasyārti hare devi nārāyaṇi namostute
(Devī Māhātmyaṁ)

O Divine Mother! You are the saviour of all who are grief-stricken and weary of this life. You remove the sorrows of the whole world. This child of yours depends upon you totally, and I offer my prostrations. O! Mother, kindly save me.

kotippū ninnaṭuttettān ammē ninnilaliyuvān
ammē, dēvi nin makkaḷē svadhāmattilettikkaṇē
ammayōṭiṅgane keñcikkēzhān vāśipiṭikkuvān
kotippū ninnaṭuttettān ammē ninnilaliyuvān

O Amma! Today I crave for the joy and the overwhelming experience of being with you. Amma, please be kind enough to hear this prayer and take all your children to their real blissful abode. Today, I am really adamant and I won't let you leave me until you grant my prayer.

|| oṁ amṛteśvaryai namaḥ ||

Mēṭam 15, April 28

Praṇāmaṁ

(Prostration)

oṁ sauśilyādi guṇākṛṣṭa jaṅgamasthāvarālaye
amṛteśvaryai namo namaḥ
amṛteśvaryai namo namaḥ

Amma! During your childhood, while you were busy with household chores, not only human beings, but also animals, trees and plants were attracted to you. The cows were delighted to let you drink milk directly from their udders. A coconut tree would drop its delicious fruit, if you became exhausted due to constant work or hunger or thirst. Again and again, I offer my morning prayers and praṇāms. Kindly give me permission to serve you.

Prabodhanaṁ

(Awakening)

harernāma harernāma harernāmaiva kevalaṁ
kalau nāstyeva nāstyeva nāstyeva gatiranyathā
(Śrī Caitanya Mahāprabhu)

Amma says:

"O my children! Look at those great ones who lived a life of devotion, chanting God's name unceasingly. Bhagavān Śrī Caitanya was one of the great amongst them. He has given "three" paths for God realization in Kaliyugam. They are Harernāma, Harernāma, Harernāma–the name of Śrī Hari.

"You may think, 'O! Hari's name! It is not for me. I am a devotee of Lord Śiva, I am a devotee of Devī or Lord Murugan or Lord Ayyappan and so on.'

"One may think, 'I am a devotee of Jesus Christ, and I have been taught that Jesus is the true God. Kāḷi is verily demonic. She dances and kills whoever possible with her sword and trident. Nothing need be said regarding Kṛṣṇa! As a child, he was a butter thief and, as a youngster, he stole the gopis' clothes while they were bathing. Not to speak of being a husband to thousands and thousands of ladies! My Jesus is the only real God.'

"Yet another may come forward and say, 'Yes, of course, Jesus may be a great prophet, But my Mohammed is the greatest and the last of all the prophets. This is what I am taught by my teachers.'

"My darling children, many of you are firm in your belief, but Amma says is that the names are different, but God is one and the same.

"Suppose we are drinking milk. We may call it by different names like pāl, dūdh, milk, dughdam, etc., Whatever may be the name, the experience is the same. But when it comes to thinking of God, the situation changes. Why? Because we don't have the necessary yearning for God.

"What Amma wants you to do is to change your mental attitude and not who it is you worship. My children! Let Amma pray for all of you."

Prayatnaṁ

(Practice)

Līla mōḷ recollects:

It was after two days of continuous yearning and waiting that the private talk with Amma had happened, and it was the fulfillment of Amma's promise that she gave during the conversation on the first night. Sitting next to Amma under a coconut tree imbibing Amma's nectarine words was indeed a unique experience. May it shine in me forever! May the sweetness of Amma's divine words eliminate the bitterness of many experiences of day-to-day life and make my life enjoyable:

"My dear daughter, we don't have to react directly to people when they give us trouble. There is an aura around those leading a life of service and love for God and aim at God-realization. The auras protect the sādhakas."

Then Amma continued saying, "The great ones are not bound to the institutions established by them. They don't have any undue sense of ownership and are always free." Amma pointed to the seashells half-burned lying under the coconut tree. "These shells seem to be retaining their form but upon closer inspection, taking them in your hand will reveal their real nature. Easily they will crumble and be made formless. The realized gurus and incarnations of God take birth and transact in human form, but they never are devoid of the cosmic vision. They live in the world but are not worldly, but godly. They can easily cross the barriers and go to the unconditioned realm. They have no fear of death, and life and death are mere child's play for them. They are never disturbed or sorrowful."

By giving in instructions, Amma, the living goddess, the guide, philosopher and friend for Līla mōḷ, was making āśraṁ life easy and smooth. The thought of basic needs of life, like easy availability of pure water, sumptuous food or warm bath, etc, were appearing to be of secondary importance, Amma being the bestower of the divine bliss as well as all needs and comforts of life.

Pratijñā

(Oath)

I will strive to make dispassion, discrimination, etc, my treasure, which will take me across the path of life without any stop.

Prārthanā

(Prayer)

ananta-saṁsāra samudra-tāra
naukāyītābhyāṁ gurubhaktidābhyāṁ
vairāgya-sāmrājyadaḥ pūjanābhyāṁ
namo namaḥ śrī gurupādūkābhyāṁ
(Gurupāduka Stotram)

O Mother, my supreme teacher, your holy feet are my lifesaving boat on the ocean of life. Kindly bestow on us the real treasure of knowledge and right understanding.

nīyallātiṅgilla vēre
śaraṇaṁ kāruṇyapūrṇṇē
nīyallātillārumammē
kāraṇa bhūtē varēṇyē
śaśvata śānti sampūrṇṇē
śaraṇaṁ kāruṇya pūrṇṇē

Amma, you are the only refuge for your children.
You are the sole cause for the cosmos.
You are the bestower of eternal peace and happiness.

|| oṁ amṛteśvaryai namaḥ ||

Mēṭam 16, April 29

Praṇāmaṁ

(Prostration)

oṁ manuṣya mṛga pakṣyādi sarva saṁsevitāṁghraye
amṛteśvaryai namo namaḥ
amṛteśvaryai namo namaḥ

Amma, from your childhood itself, the world, including plants and animals, recognized your greatness. You were served by one and all. Today, let these little children offer their humble praṇāms to you and pray for unshakable faith in your greatness.

Prabodhanaṁ

(Awakening)

tṛṇādapi sunīcēna
tarōrapi sahiṣṇunā
amāninā mānadēna
kīrttanīyaḥ sadā hariḥ
(Śrī Caitanya Mahāprabhu)

Amma says:

"The one who is humbler than a blade of grass and more enduring than a tree, the one who has completely gone beyond the evils of vanity and who is always ready to respect one and all—only such a one is qualified to be a true devotee of God.

"Many raise the question, 'Why should you start spiritual life at such a young age? There is a proper time for everything, don't you know that? Don't idle away your time singing bhajans and going to temples and āśrams and gurus.' Many are of the opinion that all spiritual disciplines must start only after 60, and they cite the example of Ajāmila. They may have heard only the name sometime, somewhere. But they haven't understood the story of Ajāmila or the message it conveys.

"Ajāmila was a Brahmin by birth. He lived the life of a traditional Brahmin until one day he happened to go to the forest for collecting articles for a homa [fire ceremony]. To his misfortune, he got attracted to a prostitute who lived in the forest. He became so attached to this woman that he never returned home. He lived with her and had many children. Finally, one day the messengers from the world of Death came to take him with them and he was so scared that he started crying out. Suddenly he remembered his last son who was yet a child and he called him by his name Nārāyaṇa.' This calling of God's name, even though not purposefully, saved him from death.

"My children, do you know how? The messengers of death waited there to take Ajāmila to the God of Death. They were about to carry out their mission, but the messengers of Mahāviṣṇu appeared on the scene. They told the messengers of Death that they had been sent by the Lord himself to take Ajāmila to their master. But the messengers of Death resisted and they fought against the messengers of Mahaviṣṇu. Finally, the messengers of Death decided to approach their master to complain. But to their astonishment, they were instructed by their master to think twice before approaching a person who utters God's name, somehow. They understood and never returned to Ajāmila.

"At Ajāmila's place, a miraculous change occurred. His place, which was a terrible hell turned into a heaven on earth. Such is the power of the name Nārāyaṇa. And do you know what happened to Ajāmila, who on his deathbed consciously witnessed the fight and arguments raised by the messengers of the two entities–Life and Death? This experience brought about in him a change for the best. He decided to discontinue his forest life with the prostitute and started a new type of austere forest life. He attained liberation from birth and death, sorrows and miseries and attained the blissful abode of Śrī Viṣṇu, Vaikuṇṭa.

"My children, do you know what the world of Vaikuṇṭa is? It is a state of mind in which sorrows and miseries have been banished forever. Now you know Ajāmila attained liberation. Think how we should live. We have to live a God-oriented life. We have to be humbler than a blade of grass and more patient than a tree. My dear children! Cast away all vanities of youthfulness, wealth and belongings. Our near and dear ones, whom we consider our own, will not remain with us forever. And our own identification with our body will only mislead us. Therefore, we should cast away 'I'-ness and respecting one and all, serve them, seeing God in each person. Only then will the Lord listen to our prayers."

Prayatnaṁ

(Practice)

Amma was singing the evening bhajans. The daughter who came to Amma recently, felt that here existed a world of reality. Amma was making life in this world enjoyable. Līla mōḷ was imbibing each and every particle of Amma's continuous nectarous singing. The sentient and nonsentient world would forget everything else and experience this divine sweetness that never disappears. New life awakens. Lying and cheating get substituted by truthfulness and love. This is what the daughter started experiencing when she came to Amma.

In later years of āśraṁ life, once Amma was giving advice regarding singing of bhajans. She and the āśramites were on a spiritual tour. A new brahmacārī was continuously singing bhajans with musical skill. Amma suddenly stopped him and told him, "I looked into your mind, it was wandering here and there. Only your lips were singing the bhajans. My son, there is no use doing such lip-service. You also had the attitude of a big singer, which is nothing to God. You will only waste your energy." This timely advice from Amma impressed all her children who were with her in the āśraṁ bus at that time. Līla mōḷ prayed to Amma, "Amma how long must we engage in various practices to be your real children? Please be kind enough to bless us."

Pratijñā

(Oath)

I will develop humility and patience in my life. I will consider these qualities as the be-all and end-all of life. I will cast away egoism and respect Godliness, present in everyone. I will serve all, seeing them as God.

Prārthanā

(Prayer)

śamādi ṣaṭka prada vaibhavābhyāṁ
samādhi dāna vrata dikṣitābhyāṁ
ramādhavānghri sthira bhakti dābhyāṁ
namo namaḥ śrī gurupādūkābhyāṁ
(Gurupāduka Stotram)

Śama, dama, uparati, titikṣā, śraddhā and samādhāna [mind control, sense control, steadfastness in dharma, forebearance, faith and one-pointedness of mind]: these six attributes are the eternal wealth of the spiritual seeker. Amma has pledged to grant samādhi to her children and Amma blesses all with devotion without deviation. Amma, I, beseech you again and again to grant me your supreme grace whenever I falter or tread the wrong path.

nilkkāttoren aśrudhārayatākave
niṣphalamākātirikkuvānāy
tāvaka sparśattālatiloru binduve
ammēyoru maṇi muttāy māttū
jīvitakkaṭalil ñānoru cippi yākave
ā maṇi muttennil jyōtissākuṁ
parama prakāśa peruṁ kaṭalāṁ tava
caraṇaṁ gatiyāy vasiccu kollāṁ

Amma! My constant tears will not be in vain if by your divine will at least a wee-drop of it turns into a shining pearl. O Amma! In this ocean of life, while I am sinking as an oyster, this little pearl will be my inner light. The light that makes the whole world shine is you! O Amma! You are an ocean of divine effulgence. I will be your humble servant and happily live my life.

|| oṁ amṛteśvaryai namaḥ ||

Mēṭam 17, April 30

Praṇāmaṁ

(Prostration)

oṁ naisargika dayātīrtha snāna klinnāntarātmane
amṛteśvaryai namo namaḥ
amṛteśvaṛyai namo namaḥ

Amma! You are the purifying holy river of compassion.
To you I bow down again and again, this happy day.

Prabodhanaṁ

(Awakening)

yaddinaṁ harisallāpa pīyūṣa rasavarjjitaṁ
taddinaṁ durddinaṁ naiva mēghachannenidurddinaṁ
(Subhāṣitaṁ)

Amma says:

"A bad day is not the one darkened by clouds and rain. A bad day is one that lacks the light of God's name. Seeing a dark day, my children, you may exclaim, 'What a bad day! What a bad day!' and go on cursing the rain and clouds and anything and everything that comes your way. This is quite natural. Amma is not finding any fault with you. You may even raise a question, 'We look outside. Our eyes can only see outside. What to do about it?' Amma agrees completely with you.

"Amma is reminded of a story. One day an old woman was very upset and was looking for something on the road. Her grandson came to her. He wanted to know why his grandma looked worried and asked her the cause of her anxiety. She told him that she had lost her sewing needle, and so both grandma and grandson together searched for the lost sewing needle. They sifted and strained each grain of sand, hoping to find the needle, but in vain. At last, the intelligent grandson asked his grandma where she had really lost the needle. She told him she lost it while she was sewing in her room. But since the room was not well lit, she had come out to search for the needle in the bright sunshine outside her home.

"The grandson was shocked at her logic. Hiding his true feelings, he said, 'Grandma, I shall help you locate the needle in the room where it was lost.' She hugged her grandson and together they started searching for the needle.

"O my children! Amma will tell you only this much. Your days and your hearts will be bright only when the light of God's name shines in you because it is God's power that illumines the sun. A bright day with good sunshine cannot substitute the divine light of God's name, which illumines the sun itself. Your heart, and your face, which mirror your heart, will not be bright even with the effulgence of thousand suns if you are not keen on glorifying God's name. Your face will be clouded, and if you happen to visit your friends, you will infect them with your melancholy. That is the reason that one of the heroic sons of Bhāratamātā, told his disciples, 'If you are gloomy and having a clouded face, shut yourself in your room. Don't go out and spread this disease of melancholy. You are not going to be benefited by it.' My children! Today, Amma will stop with this much of advice, which is sufficient for you to contemplate and proceed."

Prayatnaṁ
(Practice)

Līla mōḷ was sitting in the balcony of the small darśan temple absorbed in Amma's divine singing. Her thirst for listening to Amma's bhajans was being slaked. Amma's divine songs were echoing in her heart filling her entire being. All worries, anxieties and tensions disappeared. Amma sang the song "Sadguro pāhimāṁ jagadguro pāhimām." (O my spiritual teacher! Be kind enough to teach me and save me, you are the teacher of the whole world. Truth must guide my life; love and peace, we must have.) And then Amma reached the state of silence and peace! And Līla mōḷ, totally under the influence of the song, felt like oneness with Amma, forgetting all the worries of the world.

Subsequently this daughter came across many similar incidents during her work with the public. By then she was Swāminī Ātmāprāṇā, Swāminī Amma for the public. Once she happened to be in a house. It was late in the evening. One devotee guided her to this house. It was in connection with Amṛta Sauhṛta Yajñaṁ, which involved broadcasting Amma's message of love and service in each and every house. One house was found by her enveloped in gloom.

She and her companions remembered their guide's story of introduction. A member of this joint family was a youth who had a very good position in one of the Gulf countries. His parents were making the preparations for his wedding ceremony. Unfortunately, the poor boy met with an accident and passed away. When she came to know of the tragedy, his mother was so griefstricken that she was unable to move out of the room. She neither bathed nor ate, nor drank. She would not speak to anybody. As days passed by, her condition steadily deteriorated. An old grandmother in the house was laid up with geriatric problems. She was coughing and sneezing, gasping for breath and would frequently feel breathless. Anybody could have lost heart in this pitiable situation. But Amma's children did not lose hope. Only the young children in the house were displaying some signs of life and their interaction with the āśramites were encouraging.

The sacred lamp was lighted with chanting of mantras. A simple pūjā was performed and then bhajans commenced with the song "Bandham-illa bhanduvilla svantamallonnum" and then the mantra "oṁ namaḥ śivaya" was chanted for a while. The children participated enthusiastically in chanting the mantra. They clearly appeared to be enjoying it. When it was time for the āśramites to leave, Swāminī Amma told the children, "O! My friends! Continue chanting "oṁ namaḥ śivaya," which will make you and the others at home happy and peaceful. They did accordingly, thereby transforming the whole atmosphere from hell to heaven.

Later on, Swāminī Amma was told by the devotee, who was the head of the family, that all had turned out well after their short visit. The lady of the house, Śāntā, who never cared for food or drink or the daily routine, had come back to the normal self. When Amma returned from her tour of the West, this lady came to the āśram to receive her holy mantra from Amma. The power of Amma's love and the mantra made the river of ṣāntā's life flow again and changed it into a clean river.

Pratijñā

(Oath)

Even when the path of life is darkened by encircling
gloom, my legs shall not shake; I will stick to God's name.
I shall not forget to chant God's name incessantly and I
shall refrain from unnecessary talk and idle chatter.

Prārthanā

(Prayer)

vande nanda vraja strīṇāṁ pāda reṇumabhīkṣṇaśaḥ
yāsāṁ harikāthodgīthaṁ punāti bhuvanatrayaṁ
(Śrīmad-Bhāgavataṁ)

Uddhava, the great jñāni [sage] salutes the gopis [milkmaids], whose singing God's name purifies the three worlds.

O Amma! I'm praying, bowing down to the gopis mentally. Kindly kindle in me that great devotion that the gopis had towards Śrī Kṛṣṇa, so that I may remember God and chant His name constantly.

dēvi dēvi dēvi amṛtēśvari
caṇdikā dēvi caṇdamuṇda hāriṇi
cāmuṇḍēśvari amṛtē dēvi
saṁsāra sāgaraṁ taraṇaṁ ceyyuvān
nērāya mārgaṁ kāṭṭaṇē ammē
śānti śānti śānti lōka śānti
śānti śānti śānti duḥkha śānti
śānti śānti śānti dāridrya śānti
śānti śānti śānti nitya śānti

O Divine Mother, you who are the destroyer of evil-minded people, take me across the ocean of this life. You are the bestower of peace to the whole world, removing sorrows from the mind, removing poverty and miseries, and bestowing everlasting peace.

|| oṁ amṛteśvaryai namaḥ ||

Mēṭam 18, May 1

Praṇāmaṁ

(Prostration)

oṁ daridra janatāhasta samarpita nijāndhase
amṛteśvaryai namo namaḥ
amṛteśvaryai namo namaḥ

Amma, you, with your own food, with your own hands, fed the poor and hungry in your neighborhood. You clothed them after giving a nice cooling bath. You received in turn from your family scoldings and beatings. O Amma, to you I bow down again and again with prayers of having service-oriented mentality.

Prabodhanaṁ

(Awakening)

durlabhaṁ trayamevaitat daivānugrahahetukaṁ
manuṣyatvaṁ mumukṣutvaṁ mahā puruṣa saṁśrayaḥ
(Vivēka Cūḍāmaṇi)

Amma says:

"Darling children! Guru is instructing his disciple: 'O my son, don't be afraid. You have taken a human birth and while advancing in life naturally, you have to go through trials and tribulations that make you long for release from the bondage of mental agony. And you know, my son, a guru to a disciple is like a physician to a patient. And fortunately, you have complete faith in your guru. Your guru, of course, possesses a universal mind and a cosmic vision. In this world, human birth, desire to get liberated from the sorrows of the world, complete faith in the guru and scriptures, these three are very rare.' My children, you may be thinking that there are billions and billions of human beings in the world, so why is the guru saying that human birth is very rare?

"My children, a man can be called a 'man' only when he discriminates between right and wrong and leads his life accordingly. A selfish, narrowminded life is harmful for both the one who leads it and the whole world. You may be remembering the story of Duryodhana; what a life he lived! From the womb to the tomb, while playing, eating, fighting and celebrating, he had only one thought: 'How can I destroy the Pāṇḍavas?' His benefactors were his most evil-minded maternal uncle and brothers. His paternal uncle Vidura, who was verily a personification of dharma and Bhagavān Śrī Kṛṣṇa and his teacher Bālarāma, who were incarnations of the cosmic reality, were near and dear to Duryodhana. But he never cared to obey them and in the end, he was suffering in the battlefield from the pain and mental agony. The great Duryodhana never understood the misery he caused others, and he showered the arrows of sharp words during the last moment of his life while lying in the battlefield.

"Śrī Kṛṣṇā, after listening to him, responded by saying, 'O Duryodhana, think of your own lifeless existence darkened by evil-mindedness.' Then Duryodhana at last listened to Śrī Kṛṣṇa and admitted his defeat and said, 'Jānāmi dharmam na ca me pravṛtti, jānāmi adharmaṁ na ca me nivṛtti. ["I knew dharma, but never practiced it. I knew what was adharma but never refrained from it."] And he continued 'O Bhagavān, you must understand me when I say that it is you who made me do all this.' It was too late for him to have an awakening of discrimination. Think of the terrorists and tyrants of the present age. How nice it would be if they happened to listen to these precious words and took them into the heart. They don't realize that nature's way of responding to their evil actions is by natural disasters like floods, earthquakes, etc. O my children, will they open their eyes to see the great path of dharma trodden by the great ones of the world? You, my darling children, must determine to lead a life of sacrifice and service for the whole world. Of course, you will have to fight against adharma."

Prayatnaṁ
(Practice)

Līla mōḷ was keenly listening to Amma's divine singing in the evening. This music was sweet nectar to her ears, which would otherwise have turned deaf by the constant hearing of sharp, painful noises of the world. It was very rare to hear a sweet, nurturing word from the world.

This evening Līla mōḷ was happily diving deep in the ocean of Amma's sweet singing and while emerging, she thought, "The river of my life was becoming so disturbed," and prayed to Amma, "Amma, would you give an easy flow to this river? Make me indifferent to the many distracting noises of my past memories." How many colleagues there were who never hesitated to utter frank lies with the bad intention of putting a black mark on her academic life.

But God will always save his devotees and that is what happened to Līla mōḷ. She did not have to suffer for long. Amma took her little daughter to her bosom. Amma's divine singing again brought her mind back from these thoughts. Amma was singing the song Śakti Rūpe (O! Embodiment of Strength!) . And she finished the song by singing, "You are the omnipresent cosmic power and yet all these vanities, disputes and competitions among your children affect the whole world. O Mother, what to do about that!"

Amma finished singing, stood up and entered the small temple. This daughter had permission to follow Amma into the temple. Amma, while preparing for bhāva darśan, would spend some time with her disciples and devotees. Līla mōḷ thought, "In which aspect of God will Amma appear tonight. Will it be the mischievous boy Śrī Kṛṣṇa, or the Divine Mother who nourishes her children with her tender love and care?"

Pratijñā
(Oath)

Amma, the hardships in the path of life, and the dark hands which sometimes cause them, never could disturb you. You were always dancing on the thorns of hardships. Today, I pray and pledge that I will strive to follow you.

Prārthanā
(Prayer)

brahmānandaṁ parama-sukhadaṁ kevalaṁ jñānamūrtiṁ
dvandātītaṁ gaganasadṛśaṁ tatvamasyādi lakṣyaṁ
ekaṁ nityaṁ vimalamacalaṁ sarvvadhī sākṣi-bhūtaṁ
bhāvātītaṁ triguṇarahitaṁ sadguruṁ taṁ namāmi
(Guru Gītā)

The supreme bliss, and the absolute knowledge—that is the greatest truth to be realized. The great Vedāntic dictums like tat tvam asi ("Thou art that") are the guiding stars in the path. Sadguru, you are the eternal witness in all beings and you are the omniscient and omnipotent reality.

Kindly take me across life.

kāṇāte kara kāṇāte karayukayāṇallō

hṛdayaṁ karayukayānallō
ozhukāte bhaktiyil ozhukāte kaluṣitamāṇallō
mānasaṁ kaluṣitamāṇallō
ammē agatiyil kṛpa coriyū
ammē agatiyil kṛpa coriyū

Not seeing the shore of life, my heart is crying in pain. Not flowing in unison with the current of devotion the river of my mind is becoming very polluted. O Amma! Be merciful to your little child. Be merciful to your little child.

|| oṁ amṛteśvaryai namaḥ ||

Mēṭam 19, May 2

Praṇāmaṁ

(Prostration)

oṁ anyavaktra prabhuktānna pūrita svīya kukṣaye
amṛteśvaryai namo namaḥ
amṛteśvaryai namo namaḥ

O Amma, you are the mother of the universe who glorified that name (Jagadaṁbā) by serving one and all; by feeding them, clothing them, healing them of diseases of mind, body and intellect. My salutations to you on this bright morning, and I pray to you, Amma, to lead me from individualized approach to universal love.

Prabodhanaṁ

(Awakening)

parāñci khāni vyatṛṇat svayaṁ bhuḥ
tasmād parāṅg paśyati nāntarātman
kaścid dhīraḥ pratyagātmānaṁ aikṣat
āvṛtta cakṣūn amṛtatvaṁ icchan
(Kaṭhopaniṣad, 2-1-1)

Amma says:

"My children used to tell me, 'Amma, while meditating, our eyes and mind go here and there. Why is it so, Amma? Is there anything wrong in the mantra you gave me or in the way I chant it? I know very well, Amma, that it is because you don't have enough concern for me.'

"Amma's consoling words to those children are: 'O my children, don't cherish these wrong ideas. The great ones of the hoary past have given us enough clues regarding these things. They say that it is the Creator himself who is at fault. The Creator has created the sense organs going outwards. That's why we see what is outside and not what is inside.' Hearing this, my children may raise a question again: 'Amma, when we meditate we close our eyes and sit, yet why do we see the outside world alone?'

"Amma wants to reveal the reasons: 'O, my clever lads, remember that the real eye is not that eye made of various membranes, blood vessels, nerves and so on. It is the inner eye situated in the brain, which is a part of the mind. Of course, the outer eye and the inner eye are connected by the main optic nerve. When all these work together, we are able to see the world outside. And you know what a brave one will do? He will redirect the senses to perceive the individualized cosmic energy situated in oneself.'

"Now, my dear children may think that we thought differently about courage. We were thinking that the one who retorts in the same measure or more is brave. Amma agrees with you partially. Yes, it is bravery, but the lowest type of bravery. And, now, some of you may again question Amma, 'Amma, are they not brave who face the shower of bullets without on iota of fear?' You are correct, but not 100%. That may be a sort of courage, but the real courage is in holding back one's own instruments of perception and directing it inwards and perceiving the Real—that to be perceived. It is then and then only that you attain immortality. Amma wants to know from you, what is the fun of just taking birth and dying? Why do you want to have pain when there is no gain? Don't you want to get rid of all these unwanted miseries? If you want to do so, take the path that will lead you to eternal bliss. And Amma will be your eternal companion.'"

Prayatnaṁ

(Practice)

The devotees who came for bhāva darśan spoke with Līla mōḷ and shared some of their impressions of Amma. That time, Līla mōḷ conveyed her own experience that she had while she was at Tiruvanantapuram.

I had met the few disciples of Amma's āśram in the Tiruvanantapuram āśraṁ and the hospital where I was working as a doctor. I had an intuition that Amma is my final goal. These disciples of Amma made visits off and on to sing bhajans there.

Without direct contact, a direct relationship was being established with Amma. The burning fire of yearning to see Amma was made brighter by the poems of Śrī Ōṭṭūr Unninaṁbūritippāṭ, author of the 108 names of Amma. I remembered one special occasion of Amma's blessing. It was at the time of Śrī Śaradā Devī's (wife of Śrī Rāmakṛṣṇa) birthday celebrations. One young employee of the charitable hospital was giving a kathāprasaṅgam [storytelling by song]. He was going astray from the main theme in a very odd way. I couldn't tolerate it anymore and quietly walked out of the temple hall to sit outside in a beautiful secluded place. The beauty attracted my mind so much, and yet the thought of the odd kathāprasaṅgaṁ distracted my mind in the same measure. What followed revealed to me that all that happened was a blessing in disguise. A girl of ordinary appearance appeared suddenly and sat beside me. I asked her who she was and where she came from.

The girl replied, "I am from the nearby village, studying in seventh standard. She also mentioned her name. I wanted her to sing for me, and she sang in a most sweet and clear voice to my delightful surprise. I had not heard these songs before and after. I was feeling so much for her and asked "Where did you get these songs?" She answered, "They are from my school books." After a while she departed.

I had never met this girl before, though I regularly attended the monthly retreats at the āśram and never met again. I inquired about her to many girls of similar age and appearance, and their reply was that they never knew of such a girl. I had a strong conviction that it was Amma who had come in the form of that girl to console me. This conviction was backed up by a special incident which followed soon after.

Pratijñā

(Oath)

I shall not be dejected by adverse situations. I shall strive to concentrate on the goal and make a constant effort.

Prārthanā

(Prayer)

dhyāyāmo dhavaḷāva guṇṭhanavatīṁ
tejomayīṁ naiṣṭhikīṁ
snigdhāpāṅga vilokinīṁ bhagavatīṁ
mandasmita śrī mukhīṁ
vātsalyāmṛta varṣiṇīṁ sumadhuraṁ
saṅkīrttanālāpinīṁ
śyāmāṁgīṁ madhu sikta sūktīṁ
amṛtānandātmikām-īśvarīṁ
(Dhyāna Śloka)

We meditate on she who is robed in pure white raiment; the resplendent one who is ever-established in truth; whose benign glances beam with binding love; who is the seat of the six godly qualities; whose divine face beams with a soft, graceful smile; who incessantly showers the nectar of affection; who sings the glories of God most sweetly; who shines with the complexion of rainclouds; whose words are soaked in honey; who is immortal bliss embodied; and who is the supreme Goddess herself.

ammayen hṛdayattil vāyō
ammē hṛdayattil-ānandaṁ tāyō
ātma svarūpiṇi ammē
ātma jñāna pradāyini ammē
kāruṇya varṣiṇi ammē
divya prēma svarūpiṇi ammē
ammē en hṛdayattil vāyō
ammē hṛdayattil-ānandaṁ tāyō

O Mother, come to my heart
Fill my heart with divine bliss
O Mother, the life of my life
O Mother, the light of my heart
O Mother, the ocean of mercy
O Mother, divine love incarnate
O Mother, come to my heart
Fill my heart with divine bliss

|| oṁ amṛteśvaryai namaḥ ||

Mēṭam 20, May 3

Praṇāmaṁ

(Prostration)

oṁ saṁprāpta sarva bhūtātma svātma sattānubhūtaye
amṛteśvaryai namo namaḥ
amṛteśvaryai namo namaḥ

Amma, you could identify yourself with all living beings and refrain from all sense of duality. Your children are suffering from the serious disease of diplopia [double vision]. I am suffering because my mind is like a mad man locked up in a dark prison cell.

Amma, kindly come as a rising sun and remove the darkness of selfishness and lead me to expansion. With prayers from my heart, I again and again bow down to you.

Prabodhanaṁ

(Awakening)

dve vidye veditavye parā cāparā caiva
atha parā yayā tadakṣaraṁ adhigamyate
(Muṇḍaka Upaniṣad, 1-1-4, 5)

Amma says:

"My children, you may be under the impression that all Kēraḷites are well-educated. And Amma knows that you are very proud of it. 'Are we wrong Amma?' children would ask. Amma's answer is: 'Listen to me. There is a way to end the dispute between Amma and her children. You now listen to the music that the Divine Mother is playing for you.'

The children responded, 'But, Amma, wait, we don't have time for such a music now. We're very, very busy with our duties of the world. The only diversion we wish to have is to watch a movie on TV. Then, of course, we need time to visit doctors in medical college hospitals and super-speciality medical centers (mainly because of our life style). O Amma, there are so many other worlds of attraction for us: the movie theaters, shopping centers, five-star restaurants, etc. And Amma you are coming with this old-fashioned music on this fine morning, which we would never have listened to, but for you.'

"'O my darling children, very good. But why did you call this divine music old-fashioned? The great sages have described this music as that which sustains the whole world just as the leaves sustain a tree.'

"'O Amma, please stop! We don't have any liking for the tree or its leaves. We are the followers of the many Vīrappans [a famous bandit] in the forest.'

"'O my children, Amma doesn't like to hear you speaking this way. Vīrappan was a big terrorist hiding in the dense forest. He did all the criminal actions ever possible. He cut away all the sandalwood trees of the forest and earned a lot of money selling them. He was a challenge to his country and to his fellow countrymen and to the whole world for that matter.'

"'O Amma, you are right. We will stop instantly any unnecessary chopping of trees and plant new ones as well. But why did you blame Vīrappan alone. The author of the great epic Rāmāyana was a forest-dweller and a great robber as well in his early days.'

"'O my dear ones, you are really clever. But why did you conveniently forget to mention the differences between the two? Amma agrees with you that Vālmīki (author of the Rāmāyaṇa) was once Ratnakāran, a terrifying robber. But he later became a changed person and saved the whole world by giving them the great epic, the Rāmāyaṇa. And as for Vīrappan, you know more than I, what has happened to him. He was at last shot dead by one of the police officers. Amma doesn't want to continue with this story, but wants you to think impartially, and arrive at a proper conclusion."

Prayatnaṁ

(Practice)

Līla mōḷ sat in the temple trying to meditate while Amma started giving darśan in the divine mood of the blissful Universal Mother. She prayed, "Amma, kindly keep this mind, which normally jumps here and there like a monkey in a tree, restrained. Tie it with a rope, and, O Amma, keep the rope with you. Otherwise this monkey, which is naturally restless, will be even more so, as if it is under the influence of the strong liquor of worldliness, and also possessed by the evil spirit of desires as well as stung by the scorpion of greed and jealousy. If I don't see your shining face in the shrine of my heart, this life also will be in vain. I have given up everything else and I have come to you. Kindly give my mind one-pointed focus on your divine presence continuously. If the mind is not concentrated, then meditation is impossible. To enjoy art, music or food also requires an attuned mind. The worldly enjoyments, I don't care for, I have found them to be of transitory nature. They may give a moment's pleasure and for the rest of my life, displeasure and disease. Amma you have instructed me that within me is the non-ending treasure of bliss. The worldly enjoyment is being compared by you to that of a dog eating a bone. He goes on biting it and thinks that it is tasty and nourishing. But what happens is exactly the opposite. The dog becomes exhausted instead of stronger. He may even collapse.

Only then does he realize that he was enjoying the taste of his own blood flowing from the wounds in his mouth caused by chewing on a piece of bone.

O Amma, take this baby to your bosom. O Universal Mother, are you not my own mother also? O teacher of the whole world, are you not my teacher as well? You who are the idol and ideal of the temple of the entire cosmos, won't you shine in my heart?

Mentally talking to Amma in this strain and training the mind to focus on the name and form of her beloved deity, this daughter enjoined herself with her true mother. For quite a while she sat motionless like the steady flame of a lamp kept inside a glass case. This drop of water became completely mixed with the ocean. This little bird flying on and on upwards at last disappeared in the vast horizon. It is here that the act of meditation, the meditator and the meditated become one and the same by the grace of the universal Divine Mother.

Pratijñā

(Oath)

Each moment of life will be for chanting of the sacred name and performing service-oriented action with a sweet smiling face, a sweet word and lending a rescuing hand for those in need, and leading a life that will lead to eternal happiness.

Prārthanā

(Prayer)

mannātha śrī jagannāthaḥ
mad-guru śrī jagadguru
mad-ātmā sarva bhūtātmā

tasmai śrī gurave namaḥ
(Guru Gītā)

The guru who is my own master is the
teacher of the whole world.

The guru who makes me competent in all realms of
knowledge is the giver of knowledge to the whole world.

My own true self is the inner self of the whole cosmos.

To have this realization I bow down again
and again at my guru's sacred feet.

mānasa kṣētrattil ammaye eṅgane
śāśvatamāyi ñān vāzhikkēṇṭū
ātma-svarūpiyāṁ ammayē bandhikkān
nēḷattil prēmanūl ammayēkū

In the shrine of the heart, how can I install my Divine
Mother forever? Amma kindly give me in full length
the silk thread of love to bind you softly forever.

|| oṁ amṛteśvaryai namaḥ ||

Mēṭam 21, May 4

Praṇāmaṁ

(Prostration)

oṁ aśikṣita svayaṁ svānta sphurat kṛṣṇa vibhūtaye
amṛteśvaryai namo namaḥ
amṛteśvaryai namo namaḥ

O my Cosmic Mother, O embodiment of Śrī Kṛṣṇa, you became learned without learning and in you originated the continuous dramatization of the divine sports of Śrī Kṛṣṇa. Amma, kindly enlighten our minds with the rays of the rising sun of knowledge so that we will chant thousands and thousands of Gayatrī mantras and bow down to your feet this morning.

Prabodhanaṁ

(Awakening)

āhāra nidrā bhaya maithunaṁ caḥ
samāna metat paśubhir narāṇāṁ
jñānaṁ narāṇāṁ adhikō viśeṣaḥ
jñānena hīnaḥ paśubhir samānaḥ
(Subhāṣitam)

Āharaṁ: That which is taken inside by human beings and animals through the sense organs.

Nidrā: Sleep; when the gross sense organs sleep and become actionless, the mind and intellect perceive the whole world within themselves.

Bhayaṁ: Feelings of fear caused by identification of oneself with the body.

Maithunaṁ: The physical union of man and woman.

Ca: And; all the body functions: going to the toilet, giving birth to children, showing affection to the children, raising a family.

Samāna metat paśubhir narāṇāṁ: Physical and mental actions that are described as the same in humans and animals.

Jñānaṁ narāṇāṁ adhiko viśēṣaḥ: Knowledge about one's own inner self and the knowledge that leads to it, which makes the difference between humans and animals.

Jñānēna hīnaḥ paśubhir samānaḥ: One devoid of this knowledge is certainly animal-like.

"O My dear children, did you listen to the Vedāntic discussion that Amma just gave? Let your intellect shine like the rising sun and light up the whole world."

Prayatnaṁ

(Practice)

In the unique evening of bhāva darśan, this daughter of Amma thus prayed: "O Amma, give me knowledge, devotion, faith and save me." It was very natural for her to remain in prayer because Amma sat right in front of her eyes. And bhāva darśan was now ending. Amma got up from her seat and went to the side of each of her children who were meditating. Then she, as if jokingly, poured the holy water on the head of this daughter. Opening her eyes, this daughter had Amma's darśan. Amma was laughing and said, "Look, now Līla mōḷ has lost her bliss." Amma embraced her daughter and kissed her. When she had gone to each of the smiling meditators,

Amma took flowers in both of her hands and stood at the door of the small temple. Her children, who were her chosen singers, were singing with much fervor.

katụtta śōkamāṁ taṭattil āzhttiṭāteyenne nī
paṭutvamilla bhāgya tārakaṅgaḷillayeṅkiluṁ
kanatta cinta ninnilēkkuracciṭunnatokkeyuṁ
aṭuttu ninnariññu puñciriccu pōyiṭolle nī

Amma, don't let me fall into the waters of agony.
O Amma, this child of yours is the least amongst your children,
not having the lucky stars to support me.
I am not wise enough to master various branches of studies.
Amma yet I am having an intense yearning for you.
Don't you know that? Don't disappoint me,
by becoming indifferent to your child.
Don't leave me alone and go away.

Amma was smiling and looking benevolently at the children who were singing, as if bestowing boons of total happiness. She was showering flowers on one and all including all subtle beings present.

The door closed and Amma was no longer within sight. The song echoed around all the sentient and insentient beings and they responded by singing, "Katutta śōkamām tatattil azhttitātē enne nī."

Pratijñā

(Oath)

I pledge that I will strive to follow your example and realize the divinity within myself and within everything in existence and serve all accordingly.

Prārthanā

(Prayer)

mahāvidyā mahāmāya
mahāmedhā mahāsmṛtiḥ
mahāmohā bhagavatī
mahādevī maheśvarī
(Dēvī Māhātmyaṁ)

Mahāvidyā, mahāmāyā: The two aspects of the Divine Mother. Mahāvidyā is the greatest knowledge and mahāmayā is the illusory power that covers it.

O Mother, kindly don't delude your children with your mahāmāyā.

Mahā-medhā: the greatest intellect.
Mahā-smṛtiḥ: the faculty by which we are able to think of the past and judge and act accordingly.
Mahā-mohā: the "I-ness" and "my-ness" in one's body, wealth and family.
Bhagavatī: the Divine Mother who possesses the six divine qualities: aiśvarya, vīrya, kīrtī, śrī, jñāna and vairāgya [sovereignty, valor, fame, auspiciousness, knowledge and dispassion]
Mahādevī: the great Divine Mother who lights up the whole world with her divine radiance.
Maheśvarī: The Divine Mother who is the Goddess, even for the trinity: the creator, sustainer and destroyer of the world.

O my Amma, please be kind enough to
protect me, your little child.

entineniykkanya cintakaḷ-aṁbikē
nin-pada cintanaṁ mātram-ēkū
ellāṁ ennammayaṇenna bodhaṁ nalki
ennil ninnajñānaṁ nīkkiyāluṁ

O Amma, why do you give me many thoughts? Give me the continuous remembrance of your sacred feet only. Amma, you are everything that exists, kindly make me aware of that.

|| oṁ amṛteśvaryai namaḥ ||

Mēṭam 22, May 5

Praṇāmaṁ

(Prostration)

oṁ acchinna madhurodāra kṛṣṇa līlāusandhaye
amṛteśvaryai namo namaḥ
amṛteśvaryai namo namaḥ

O Amma! The continuous performance of various household chores and meditation on the divine sport of the child Kṛṣṇa were completely filling the days of your childhood. O Amma! You are verily Śrī Kṛṣṇa, which I understand by contemplating on your divine life.

Prabodhanaṁ

(Awakening)

vidyādadāti vinayaṁ
(Subhāṣitam)

Amma says:

"O my darling children, humility is often taken to be cowardice and this misconception is verily the result of vanity and lack of real understanding. Can you for a while listen to great hymns in Malayāḷam? From those who are 'devas,' you can hear the vanity of 'goodness,' whereas 'asuras' are always boasting to be physically mighty and great in other aspects in their own way. The various conditionings of both good and bad slowly form a fortress in our heart. As if in the wild animal, the various tendencies freely have their play. 'God kindly save me from the wilderness of pride and egoism' is a very relevant prayer to make. The vanity of goodness is harmful; let us see how it takes us away from reality. Those who are good-natured are caught up in thoughts like, 'How great I am in charity and ceremonial worship! I am there in the front row in the great gathering of "big shots."' These people go on spending money to earn name and fame. If someone needy and downtrodden happens to be a visitor in the home and begs for help, he will be immediately chased away empty-handed. These 'big devotees' would go to the temple every day but fail totally to worship God in human form and even despising his fellowmen. They would even go to the extent to think that they are even bigger than God and give 'great divine instructions.' This vanity is the result of incorrect and incomplete understanding and experiencing truth.

"Have you thought of the impact of Śrī Kṛṣṇa's worship of Govardhana Hill? Was it not for teaching Indra, the god of mental activities? Understand that even the gods in the form of the Creator, Sustainer, and Destroyer (Brahmā, Viṣṇu and Śiva in their conditional forms) would find it difficult to cross the barrier of this egoism. Now let us leave alone those of good tendencies to be with the ones who are boasting of their misconceptions and unrighteousness. The hymns of the Hari nāma kīrtana have given the identity of them. They would never hesitate to quarrel with anyone to establish their supremacy and easily fall into the deep well of their own evil doings and get lost. Suppose someone would volunteer to save them. Not only would they refuse the help, but they would try to pull the person trying to help, down to their state as if they are possessed by an evil spirit–the demon of egoism!

"O my children, understand that if you would have peace of mind you must cultivate humility and concern for others. The true education aims at peace and happiness."

Prayatnaṁ
(Practice)

After the bhāva darśan had finished, Amma sat down in the courtyard of the āśraṁ, where the feathery leaves of the coconut trees, together with the moonlight, were painting beautiful shades. Devotees also sat down beside Amma.

Līla mōḷ, getting attuned to the sound of the ocean, sat beside a coconut tree near the large backwater pond while listening to the divine conversation of Amma with the devotees. She asked them, 'Don't you want to sleep?' Amma's children only wished to be near her, keeping awake. Amma does not differentiate between night and day when she is at her spiritual ministration. Likewise, the dirty ponds formed by the backwaters, which also served as the toilets of the neighboring residents, were to Amma as if similar to the holy water of the sacred rivers. Her children wanted to follow Amma's example. They have learned to sit anywhere possible and to lie down and sleep anywhere as well. If food ran out–which happened frequently on bhāva darśan nights–they go without food, but not with any feelings of frustration at having missed dinner. The bliss they enjoyed in Amma's presence was more than enough to make them forget the world for the time being. The residents of the āśraṁ would invite the visitors into their own huts to take rest, and they would go out under the roof of the sky.

"Give, that you would receive. Bow down, that you would rise high." This Amma's disciples realized in her divine presence. Mother Nature and Amma, the living Cosmic Mother, were inspiring one and all to go beyond the limitations of the body.

Pratijñā

(Oath)

I shall try to be humble and overcome all the negative feelings and rivalry and never react impatiently.

Prārthanā

(Prayer)

yā devi sarva bhūteṣu
śaktirūpeṇa saṁsthitā
namastasyai namastasyai
namastasyai namo namaḥ
yā devi sarva bhūteṣu
dayārūpeṇa saṁsthitā
namastasyai namastasyai
namastasyai namo namaḥ
(Devī Māhātmyaṁ)

The Universal Mother is omnipresent and manifests as the power behind the universe in three ways: sattvika [rest and peace], rajāsika [activity and bondage] and tamāsika [inactivity and distraction]. When in sattvika form, she is Śrī Sarasvatī; in rajāsika form, she is the Śūlinyādi devatas, and in her tamāsika form she is the Śivadutyādi devatas. Salutations to the Divine Mother who is manifest and yet beyond all manifestations.

The Universal Mother manifests as compassion in beings in three ways. Sattvika, the highest form of compassion, is being compassionate to those who are righteous and are having adversities in life. The second type, rajāsika, is being compassionate to those who are wealthy but caught in danger. The third and lowest type, tamāsika, is the compassion shown towards those who are cruel and unkind when they are in trouble.

Salutations to the Divine Mother, who is manifesting as the threefold forms of compassion. Salutations to the Mother who is the cosmos and who is beyond all manifestations in the form of Absolute Knowledge.

amma sadguru rūpiṇi amma
amma sadgunā rūpiṇi amma
amma vedānta rūpiṇi amma
amma vedārtha rūpiṇi amma

Amma is my greatest teacher.
Amma is the highest manifestation of
the three aspects of the world.
Amma is the visible form of knowledge of the Vedas.
Amma is the teacher who imparts the highest Vedic wisdom.
O Amma, I surrender all my day's experiences
and pray for a bright tomorrow.

|| oṁ amṛteśvaryai namaḥ ||

Mēṭam 23, May 6

Praṇāmaṁ

(Prostration)

oṁ nandātmaja mukhāloka nityotkaṇṭhita cetase
amṛteśvaryai namo namaḥ
amṛteśvaryai namo namaḥ

Amma, allow me to meditate on you this morning as the divine child who appeared to be the ardent seeker of Śrī Kṛṣṇa with prayers of complete faith in you. You are my ideal of divine love and seeking of God without any break whatsoever.

Prabodhanaṁ

(Awakening)

vidyādhanaṁ sarvadhanāl pradhānaṁ
"Wealth of wisdom is the greatest wealth."

Amma says:

"Many who come to Amma complain, 'Amma, we are so poor and suffering from lack of means. Others are so vain and eager to show off their possessions.' 'Amma, our Toyota must be replaced by a Mercedes. It's old, and our son is complaining. Can we buy a new luxury car?' Generally speaking, all are eager to accumulate material wealth. They go on earning money by hook or crook, either in their own country or abroad. They have a large bank balance, yet they are not satisfied due to lack of understanding of the real nature of material possessions. Will they keep anything permanently with them?

"Amma remembers a story of a boat race. My children may be thinking of the usual boat races in the backwaters during festivals, but this boat race was of a different nature. The theme was 'As much speed, so much land.' Meaning, the winners would get as much land as they could cover as long as they could finish by sunset. This prize attracted many contestants. Everyone wanted to participate. Many started practicing the art of rowing day and night. The contestants earned as much land as they could. The race was becoming more and more popular, and the audience was also increasing. One day the racing was very special—one of the participants was exceptionally speedy. The audience was lost completely in watching him. Now it was almost sunset. 'He's going to win more land than anyone before him!' the people remarked. But while they eagerly waited to congratulate him, they saw his boat gradually tipping and then starting to sink.

"My children you may be wondering, how did all this happen? Too much greed makes one deluded and delusion leads to destruction and disaster."

Prayatnaṁ

(Practice)

The āśramites came to Amma to have the real education and to know God, which is nothing but true existence, knowledge and bliss. Most of them had good academic education and could easily become well-settled in family life, but the direct and indirect experiences in life turned them into spiritual aspirants, seeking to know what is ever-abiding, lasting. Wealth and material possessions alone cannot make one really happy and content in life—and not to speak of a peaceful death! More possessions, more troubles—wife, children and relatives come forward, each one competing with others to get a bigger share of the wealth.

Look at any household; we can see this is what is happening, money counts most. Līla mōḷ recollected a scriptural story in this connection. This story is from the Bikṣu Gītā of the Śrimad-Bhāgavatam. The main character of the story is a wealthy householder who was very miserly. He cared for nothing else but to earn money and wouldn't spend it even for family, not to mention receiving guests or charities. His wife and children and all others hated him. Finally he lost all his money and became a beggar. The share that should have gone to the king was acquired by the officials. Floods and droughts took away many of his possessions. Finally, his wife and children, who were ill-treated by him all the while, left him for good. When he was left alone, he had an inner awakening. He could now clearly see that it was his greed and miserliness that brought him so much suffering and loss. Now his mind was prepared to accept what came to him. He thought he could become a sannyāsi and lead the rest of his life in peace. At last he could rise above his craving for material possessions because of his awareness of the everlasting wealth.

He did not care for prestige and personal comforts. He moved on and on alone without any possessions. One day he was so thirsty and hungry, having not eaten for days, he wanted to sit and eat what food he got by begging. He was surrounded by naughty children who teased him and threw stones at him. They even urinated in his food.

However, the sannyāsi could now remain calm and untroubled by the external disturbances. He had perfect mental balance. He thought, "When the mind is established in higher values, past, present and future, here and hereafter, present no tension." Thus, desiring nothing, he lead the rest of his life in peace and attained liberation.

Līla mōḷ recollected this story often after starting to lead an āśraṁ life and going through various experiences. Amma is the only true solace and true happiness. Līla mōḷ remembered Amma's advice: "My daughter, you must concentrate on scriptural studies." In the āśraṁ Vedānta Vidyālayaṁ [Vedānta School], Kaṭhopaniṣad was being taught. Līla mōḷ proceeded to the Vedānta Vidyālayam in response to the bell ringing.

Pratijñā

(Oath)

I shall try my very best to concentrate my mind to learn
the higher truths and practice them in my daily life.

Prārthanā

(Prayer)

sāvidyā paramā muktēr
hētu bhūtā sanātanī
saṁsāra bandha-hētuśca
saiva sarveśvareśvarī
(Devī Māhātmyaṁ)

The Divine Mother is the supreme knowledge. In the Vedas, knowledge is classified into two types: the highest wisdom and the informative knowledge. The informative knowledge includes any academic teaching, scriptural or secular. The supreme knowledge is considered direct perception of the supreme truth shining in every being which has no change at any time. Divine Mother is that supreme knowledge and directs us towards attaining the truth.

O My Divine Mother, make this little child
of yours realize your supreme nature

pātālattil tānupōvukillent
rājapattaṁ tallippōvukilentmaṇṇuṁ viṇṇuṁ alanna tṛppādaṁ
innenikkitā svantamayallō
kuttarellāruṁ pōvukilent
prānaninnenne piriyukilent
ente jīvanaṁ ammaye kanṅil
kaṇṭuvallō ini kāttirikkāṁ

Amma, I may go through various experiences good and bad
in the world, yet I must hold on to you. Kindly, O my savior,
teach the whole world to abide in the ever-existing reality.

|| oṁ amṛteśvaryai namaḥ ||

Mēṭam 24, May 7

Praṇāmaṁ

(Prostration)

oṁ govinda viprayogādhi dāva dagddhāntarātmane
amṛteśvaryai namo namaḥ
amṛteśvaryai namo namaḥ

Amma, this morning let me think of you and prostrate at your lotus feet with prayers of attaining a higher mental state by continuous contemplation on your yearning and striving for God in the form of Śrī Kṛṣṇa. Let me progress towards you, the Universal Mother.

Prabodhanaṁ

(Awakening)

svalpam-apyasya dharmasya trāyate mahato bhayāt
(Bhagavad-Gītā, 2-40)

Amma says:

"Dear children, remember worldly possessions alone cannot make one happy and fearless. From dawn to dusk you strive and strive for worldly goods and earn as much as you can from the world. You may succeed. But every moment you are unhappy and tense. As days pass by, life is filled with worries and finally death overtakes you. As death comes you have to bid adieu to all your belongings. Throughout your life you have been enjoying in all possible ways. Yet could you for a moment be free of mental tension and thoughts of disease and death? These days almost everything that you consume is adulterated with various harmful chemicals. Natural ways of cooking with firewood, use of medicinal herbs, etc, are totally ignored. And most of you look forward to acquiring only commercial products that will give momentary ease and pleasure and then suffering and ill health later in life. This external nature affects your personality. You are never calm and composed. Tolerance and acceptance give way to impatience and terrorism and underground activities. O my children, Amma is so worried thinking where this type of life will take you. Come back to Mother Nature. Learn and practice the eternal values."

Prayatnaṁ

(Practice)

Līla mōḷ really admired the life in the āśram. The pleasure-oriented life of the world got replaced by the happy, austere and simple life of the āśram. Meeting Amma's first disciples there, she remembered:

Once Amma's disciples presented the Hari Katha [storytelling by song] of Śrī Rāmakṛṣṇa in the hospital prayer hall. Their performance had a marvelous effect on her mind. This program had been preceded by one of a similar nature on Śrī Śāradā Devī during the Śrī Śāradā birthday celebrations in the Neṭṭayam Ashram. This was in December and was of very inferior quality. Soon after, in February, during Śrī Rāmakṛṣṇa's birthday celebrations, she could hear the divine rendering of the story of Śrī Rāmakṛṣṇa with soul-stirring melodious music. The program presented by Amma's children was so great that it could remove all unpleasant memories of the previous program (which was rendered by one of the hospital staff members). It was as if Amma had directly made her children do it to inspire Līla mōḷ. And Līla mōḷ had sufficient evidence to think so. Her belief was Amma had come to her as a young girl singing the mysterious bhajans, offering her soothing presence,

and soon after had sent her children to give a real devotional Hari Katha program. Amma's palpable presence was filling the place, and Līla mōḷ, who was still waiting to be with Amma, wondered when and how she would again meet Amma. Certainly she was going through a period of uncertainty and dilemma. The only solace was Amma's subtle presence and a long series of divine experiences she had from Amma.

Pratijñā

(Oath)

I will progress towards the goal through the path trodden
by Amma with the help of all that she has taught.

Prārthanā

(Prayer)

na śatruto bhayaṁ tasya
dasyuto vā na rājataḥ
na śastrānalatoyaughāt
kadācit saṁbhaviṣyati
(Devī Māhātmyaṁ)

Amma! Scriptures teach that the one who takes refuge in the divine will not have any fear from rulers, rivals or weapons, fire or water. Amma, this child has none but you. Kindly save me.

ammayen hṛdayattil vāyo ammē
hṛdayattil-ānandaṁ tāyō
śakti svarūpiṇi ammē nitya-
mukti pradāyini ammē
śatrusaṁ hāriṇi ammē nityaṁ
bhakti pradāyini ammē

ammayen hṛdayattil vāyo ammē
hṛdayattil-ānandaṁ tāyō

O Mother, come to my heart.
Fill my heart with thy bliss.
O Mother, the strength of my life!
O Mother, the goal of my life!
O Mother, remover of enmity!
O Mother of divine love!
O Mother, come to my heart.
Fill my heart with thy bliss.

|| oṁ amṛteśvaryai namaḥ ||

Mēṭam 25 May 8

Praṇāmaṁ

(Prostration)

oṁ viyoga śoka saṁmūrcchā muhuḥ patita varṣmaṇe
amṛteśvaryai namo namaḥ
amṛteśvaryai namo namaḥ

O Amma, with humble prostrations to you, I pray to make my mind calm and composed so that I may perceive your greatness and make you my ideal. Amma, you were born perfect, yet you went through rigorous spiritual disciplines to set an example for the world.

Prabodhanaṁ

(Awakening)

dharmo rakṣati rakṣitaḥ
(Vedic Scriptures)

Amma says:

"O my children, for many of you the word dharma has become flavorless. This indifference to discipline has become so disastrous, even more than natural disasters. Many think that to speak of universal discipline is not proper. Dharma is not sectarianism, but those universal laws sustain the world. The five great causative principles that contribute to create the universe have their functions: earth is the grossest principle and contributes to form the substratum of the planet; wind composes the five types of prāṇa [life-force] residing in each individual; water is cooling and nourishing; fire and light illumine the universe and create the awareness of its existence; space is the most subtle, the element in which the planets and stars themselves exist. What Amma is explaining is that every simple thing in the world has its own part to play. The five elements have the subtler force behind them.

"My children, you may ask what is the dharma for human beings? There are four aspects: truth, charity, compassion and control of the senses and mind. When the cosmic cycle starts, dharma has these four limbs. With each cycle one limb is removed. In Kali Yuga, dharma has only one limb. Only truth remains. This truth we have to adhere to completely and practice ceaselessly."

Children: "Amma now it is very clear to us. The various irregularities that we find in society, like cheating and other negative tendencies are a result of not practicing truth."

Amma: "I agree with you. But my children, remember that the Himālayas of unrighteousness will disappear when the sun of dharma starts shining. You must not become indifferent to the observance of dharma. You must be on the path of dharma and be victorious in life. Amma is with you."

Prayatnaṁ

(Practice)

After finishing the morning routine of spiritual practices, Līla mōḷ was happily engaged in activities like doing Amma's laundry. The washing stone was near the wash basin. The crows had their meals on the wash basin and they used the washing stone as their toilet! Līla mōḷ knew very well the mischief the crows would do if she left the washed clothes on the stone even for a little while. The crows are supposed to be scavengers by nature, but, alas, these scavengers remind one of modern social workers–little service and more fortune. Līla mōḷ was fed up with these scavengers and was becoming more and more conscious of their mischief. She spread Amma's holy white clothes to dry before she went to meet the two colleagues who had come to visit her. While conversing with the two senior doctors, Līla mōḷ told them that she never wanted to return to her former position, and they would soon have to find another doctor to replace her. The swāmiji in charge of the hospital had sent a telegram telling her to return, to which Līla mōḷ had replied in the negative, quoting from the *Gospel of Śrī Rāmakṛṣṇa*: "The ship which has gone to the black waters never returns." Amma was amused by this.

Meanwhile Amma was going to the seashore to meditate in the evening. Līla mōḷ and the two doctors joined the group. The seashore was shining in the golden twilight. The horizon was as if waiting for the setting sun. All meditated with Amma.

Amma returned to the āśraṁ when it was bhajan time. She sat in the right side of the kaḷari and sang in a divine mood. All were immersed in Amma's singing.

vandikkunnēnammē ennil nṛttam-āṭuvān
vandanīya prabhē vannaṭi paṇiyunnēn

This song attracted Līla mōḷ so much, she was completely absorbed. After bhajans, Amma talked with the doctors and lovingly served dinner. Afterwards they took leave of Amma. She was lying under the ñāval tree on the bare earth. Līla mōḷ sat at her feet. Amma's face was radiant with unusual luster and was serious and deep in hue. This face reminded Līla mōḷ of that night when Amma had appeared to her when she was in bed half-asleep.

Amma turned to Līla mōḷ and told her, 'I doubt that they will call for you any more...'

Looking at Amma, Līla mōḷ sat spellbound without any words.

Pratijñā

(Oath)

I will not step back from the right path. My life will be a constant endeavor to follow Amma.

Prārthanā

(Prayer)

akhaṇḍa maṇḍalakāraṁ
vyāptaṁ yena carācaraṁ
tat-padaṁ darśitaṁ yena
tasmai śrī gurave namaḥ
(Guru Gītā)

The indivisible consciousness filling the whole universe, may I perceive with guru's grace. Amma, I offer myself at your feet and pray that you lead me to reach the goal.

etrayō sandhyakaḷ maññupōyi
etrayō rātridinaṅgaḷuṁ pōyi
etrayō gāna-sumaṅgaḷ-ammē
tṛppādaṁ tēṭi viṭarnnu vīṇu
guru-caraṇa śaraṇāgatar makkaḷ
guru-caraṇa sēvanaṁ jīvanaṁ
guru-caraṇāṁbuja prēma-bhakti
ammē śrī sadgurō makkaḷkkēkū

O! How many twilights, nights and days have passed by? O! How many songs are offered at your feet by your children who are totally depending on you, serving in their full capacity? Amma, bestow divine love to us.

|| oṁ amṛteśvaryai namaḥ ||

Mēṭam 26, May 9

Praṇāmaṁ

(Prostration)

oṁ sārameyādi vihita śuśrūṣā labdha buddhaye
amṛteśvaryai namo namaḥ
amṛteśvaryai namo namaḥ

O Amma, while doing works like collecting grass for the cows in your childhood, you were fully immersed in Śrī Kṛṣṇa, and you used to fall on the ground unconscious of the external world. Animals like dogs, ducks and snakes used to come near you and take care of you and awaken you. This type of intense yearning and struggling was to set an example for the world.

Prabodhanaṁ

(Awakening)

adveṣṭā sarva bhūtānāṁ maitraḥ karuṇa eva-ca
nirmamo nirahaṅkāraḥ sama-duḥkha sukha-kṣamī
santuṣṭaḥ satataṁ yogī yatātmā dṛḍha niścayaḥ
mayyarpita mano buddhiḥ yo mad bhakta saḥ me priyaḥ
(Bhagavad-Gītā, chapter 12, verses 13-14)

Amma says:

"My children, today Amma will tell you the answer to a commonly asked question. 'Amma, many who appear to be devotees externally, wearing external marks and visiting centers of ritualistic worship of various religions, singing and observing many customs, are they not really so?' The 12th chapter of the Bhagavad-Gītā reveals the nature of ideal devotion. You may read and contemplate on these words carefully.

"Many are indifferent to devotion and spirituality because of ignorance though they are qualified to become real devotees. They often did not have chances to meet real devotees. Amma would like to tell you a story:

"One person used to sit under a banyan tree in a temple yard repeating God's name. He thought that by calling God by name, God would appear before him. Days passed by and nothing happened, though he was considered to be a great devotee. One day he saw a couple who used to visit the temple regularly going to some other place. They appeared to be carrying certain things for someone. This continued for some time. The man was curious. They used to be very silent, not talking much to anyone. One day, he could see the couple coming back running with unusual joy, which they expressed by calling out 'We have seen God!' repeatedly. The so-called devotee enquired, 'I saw you going out and yet you are returning so soon. What are you shouting with so much joy?' Hearing him they came back to the world and answered him. 'We could see God.' 'How is that,' he asked, 'I have been calling for such a long time. Never could I see. How could you see where were you going with a bag in your hand?'

"They answered, 'A sick and lonely old man lives in the nearby valley. He was hungry and happened to fall on the road one day. We saw him and did nursed him back to health and took him back to his hut and fed him. No one used to come to him because they thought he would infect them. We could give him the necessary care and medicine and bring food for him. We had heard even God would appear in the form of food before one who is hungry. We could do this everyday in a spirit of worship, and today when we saw the old man healthy and happy, we went into a state of rapture. We both experienced the divine joy. It was the palpable presence of God. We could see God everywhere when we were running back to the temple.'

"The 'devotee' could not understand that he was not on the right path. He was neglecting his duties in the name of seeking God.

"Amma would like to tell you that God is there where there is love and service. 'My own good' alone is not a good attitude. God is an ocean of love and mercy. God is in everyone in the form of love. To injure anyone unnecessarily is not good. Social work done with a selfish motive or egoism will not serve the purpose. To serve one and all seeing God in them should be the aim of work."

Prayatnaṁ

(Practice)

Seeing Amma talking with devotees sitting under the coconut tree in the courtyard, Līla mōḷ approached. What she heard was soul-stirring. Amma was explaining and gesturing to the surroundings, drawing the devotees' attention to the ambiance. "Look, God is not separate from all this. He doesn't sit somewhere high. But alas! The vast majority doesn't usually perceive this truth. It is as if a door is closed, obstructing the vision. Only the strong wind of love for God can open the door." These revelations given by Amma remained with Līla mōḷ for a long time and inspired her to remember an anecdote:

I was traveling in a bus and started thinking of Amma. It was before becoming a member of the āśram, and I did not have direct contact with Amma. I had heard that Amma could cross the barrier of "I and mine" and love all as her own. What I thought was that Amma's greatness may be due to consciously practicing the ideal of selfless love.

One day soon after joining the āśram, I was sitting in Amma's room alone with Amma. She instantly started talking about her childhood. She was in a special divine mood. She said, "Amma, from six years onwards, started composing and singing songs to God. While doing household chores, Amma never forgot to chant "Kṛṣṇa Kṛṣṇa" even for a moment. While walking, a mantra with each step was the rule. If Amma forgot by chance, she would step back, chant, then walk forward."

Then Amma talked about Devī worship: "The Divine Mother of the Universe was like Amma's own dear mother, and Amma became like her little darling baby. Once Amma told her, 'O Mother, won't you play your vīna for me?' Amma persisted asking and crying until losing all external consciousness. Then Amma could hear the divine music from the Divine Mother's vīna. Another time, while immersed in meditation, Amma again lost external consciousness and fell in the backwaters. The Divine Mother came in the form of a fisherwoman and took Amma in a boat to the shore. It was at this time Amma awakened to the outside world and recognized what had happened.

"Kṛṣṇa, my playmate in childhood at that time, was as if hiding in Amma, but Amma wished to see Bhagavān on the outside. So, Bhagavān came to Amma crawling on his knees as baby Kṛṣṇa as if to his mother. Amma told him, 'O Bhagavān, come to me not as my baby but as my father.' But he never came in that form."

Amma was completely lost in a rare mood of divine bliss with teardrops in the corners of her eyes. She remained in that mood for a long time. As she came back to external consciousness, Amma said, "My darling child, this type of divine love will not be present in anyone just by spiritual practice."

The words opened my inner eyes and the thoughts which had flashed in my mind Amma had known. This revelation today is the answer for that, that Amma's greatness is not the result of her spiritual practices because it is impossible to do so. It is due to the rare phenomenon of God incarnating in human form, the form of a loving mother to the world.

Pratijñā

(Oath)

This evening, I will begin practicing the awareness
of the truth that Amma is the personification
of the all-pervading consciousness.

Prārthanā

(Prayer)

amṛtapurī bāhyāntare vā brahmasthāna sevāsthāne
sarvatra sadāhyamṛtānandaṁ yadihṛdayāmṛtāṁ paśyati cet

O Amma! Who resides in the heart of everyone! You will
give the realization of your highest nature to those who
strive to see you in their hearts and everywhere else.

nityaṁ satyaṁ tava nāmaṁ nityaṁ mananaṁ tava-mantraṁ
varadābhayadayāṇennamma śubhadāsukhadā mama mātā

O Amma, make your children immersed in your real
nature and in your holy name, and let them realize
that you would grant the boons of fearlessness and a
blissful life and attainment of the highest goal of life.

|| oṁ amṛteśvaryai namaḥ ||

Mēṭam 27, May 10

Praṇāmaṁ

(Prostration)

oṁ prema bhakti balākṛṣṭa prādurbhāvita śārṅgiṇe
amṛteśvaryai namo namaḥ
amṛteśvaryai namo namaḥ

Amma, the one-pointed devotion to God and constant effort to realize the highest truth in the form of Śrī Kṛṣṇa made it possible for you to have his presence, constantly being aware of your total identification with him. In this serene morning I beg you to grant me real love for God.

Prabodhanaṁ

(Awakening)

sātvasmin parama-prema-rūpā
(Nārada Bhakti Sūtram)

Amma says:

"O my darling children, God is our own real being, which we will realize when we become totally identified with the inner self. Religion is the way to reach this goal. God is never distant from us. He is the all-pervading existence. He is there everywhere in every being as the life-giving energy. This the seers call oṁkāra. You, my children, are in reality the essence of the Oṁ, of which Amma urges you to be aware. Know that Amma will strive to the maximum to awaken you to this truth. Will you listen to Amma's call?"

Children: "O Amma, we will listen to your call. But oṁkāra and the real nature that is the all-pervading consciousness remain unfamiliar to us because of our negligence to the reality. We never consciously thought of leading a life aware of its real purpose."

Amma: "Amma is happy when you admit this serious mistake of forgetting yourself and going astray. The boat of your life is very unsteady and will fail to take you across if you are careless in steering towards the goal. You often run like a horse without reins through this life. You dream of having a sumptuous birthday feast in a ship which is sinking. How long can you live on sensual pleasures? When death comes, to what will you cling to?"

Children: "Amma, we never thought in this way. Kindly open our eyes and lead us."

Amma: "Amma will wait for you, my dear children. May you find the real source of happiness. Amma is never tired of working for the whole world."

Prayatnaṁ

(Practice)

Līla mōḷ joined the āśram after a few months of waiting anxiously for Amma and working in the hospital, after she had met Amma for the first time. It was then she had received a consoling telephone call from Dr. Devaki. Līla mōḷ was feeling the changes occurring inside and outside after she had met Amma. Dr. Devaki was telling her, "Amma is coming to Abhedāśramam and will be staying there for three days. Take leave from work and be with Amma. Don't fail to do so for any reason."

This friendly order she could not carry out fully outwardly because of the duties in the hospital, but her mind was with Amma. On the evening of the third day, Līla mōḷ could manage to reach the venue where Amma was giving darśan. It was verily a pilgrimage to Amma which changed the course of her life.

She had to join the big line of persons waiting for Amma's darśan. She felt a little sad to wait in a line to meet her own mother! The twilight was coming and she was getting nearer and nearer to Amma. It was Amma's final darśan day in this āśram and she had waited for this day. She wondered how Amma would greet her. "Will Amma recognize me and will all my doubts and problems get solved?" she thought. One by one all were going to Amma and were as if becoming one with Amma for the time being; the individual and cosmic personalities becoming one and the same without differentiation. This light was awakening in Līla mōḷ, a sort of rare happiness of a new awakening.

Amma was not showing any signs of recognizing her. Līla mōḷ was also received as any other in the line, and she was left to herself while she sat, completely lost in Amma. She forgot all about her doubts about her future life which she had hoped to solve by Amma's darśan. She surrendered totally to Amma and sat near Amma for a while. It was at this moment that Amma turned to her and looked at her. This look of love and kindness she felt would sustain her. She had waited for Amma's words and she heard, "Daughter, how many members are there in your āśram?" This question happened to be the words to open the closed door of her future life.

Her answer was, "I have not become a member of the āśram, Amma. I am working in the hospital; that is all." The remaining portion of Amma's divine conversation that day, though sounding quite casual, had solved Līla mōḷ's doubts about her future life and helped her to reach Amma soon.

Pratijñā

(Oath)

This little child of yours, O Amma, will feel blessed by any of your looks, words and little spiritual awakenings. I shall always strive to be in tune with you.

Prārthanā

(Prayer)

śaraṇaṁ śaraṇaṁ parameśvari
śaraṇaṁ śaraṇaṁ jagad-īśvari
abhayaṁ dehi akhileśvari
āśrayaṁ dehi amṛteśvari

O Supreme Mother, protect us. Are you not the mother of the whole world? Give me refuge and the mind to depend on you.

amṛteśvari amṛteśvari amṛteśvari jay
amṛtānandamayi sadguru jay
brahmānandini sad-ānandini amṛtānandini jay
amṛtānandamayi jagad-guru jay
aṁbā aṁbā jaya jagad-aṁbā
amṛtānandamayi jagad-aṁbā

O Amma! You who lead your children to the real goal of life, I pray for total devotion to you. Amma, with these prayers let me finish this day.

|| oṁ amṛteśvaryai namaḥ ||

Mēṭam 28, May 11

Praṇāmaṁ

(Prostration)

oṁ kṛṣṇā loka mahāhlāda dhvasta śokāntarātmane
amṛteśvaryai namo namaḥ
amṛteśvaryai namo namaḥ

O Amma, let me start this day praying for unalloyed devotion to you. You are the personification of the highest form of love for God because you are one with the Supreme, which is nothing but never-ending bliss.

Prabodhanaṁ

(Awakening)

kaḥ śokaḥ komohaḥ ekatvam-anupaśyataḥ
(Īśāvāsya Upaniṣad, 7)

Amma says:

"My children, listen to the words of the Mother Veda: Today the reason for unhappiness and misery will be revealed. No one in the world is beyond sorrow. Material wealth does not bring happiness, and poverty naturally is considered to be the cause of misery. Children may rarely add to the happiness of the parents, and having no children is the cause of frustration. Think of the professional career. The advocate may look at the doctor's profession as better than his, but the doctor may be preoccupied with the idea that to become an engineer would be better. 'Then I could have enjoyed life better.' Teachers are always troubled by the students who are disobeying them. And not to mention those who are in the field of administration. The Sword of Damocles is always hanging over the head of those in charge. The ladies who are at home looking after the household always look upon their friends who are employed as more fortunate than them. Lack of bodily health brings pain and misery, and when the body becomes healthy other problems crop up. Hunger is a great pain and a sumptuous feast also does not make one really happy. There is no end to this type of unhappiness for you, my children. The funny thing is that real sorrow is something else. Never even once did you enjoy real bliss in life. This must be the real sorrow. To know God, who is infinite bliss, is the way to cross the ocean of unhappiness."

Prayatnaṁ

(Practice)

One day at the āśraṁ Līla mōḷ happened to remember one of those nights in Tiruvanantapuram. It was after meeting Amma and while waiting to become her disciple. Naturally the separation from Amma was like a scorching summer for Līla mōḷ.

One night she could feel the cooling touch of Amma. Amma was sitting near her bed while she was half-asleep, and Amma's dark face was beaming with a divine light. It was not by senses she felt but by the sense beyond the sense perception. She vividly felt that by Amma's divine touch her vital energy was becoming awakened and rising upwards. This experience filled her entire being. When she awoke and Amma was nowhere to be seen, she wondered what could have been the import of this experience.

It was after she became an āśramite and lived with Amma that she clearly understood the meaning of that wonderful episode. When her senior colleagues came to take her back, Amma had spent much time with them. After they left, Amma was lying down under the ñāval tree lost in her own world. Her face had the same appearance as that of that night. This sight brought the feeling to Līla mōḷ that her life is totally connected, never to become separated from Amma any more. This thought brought great happiness and consolation to her.

Pratijñā

(Oath)

Let my life become a continuous effort to
become one with the everlasting bliss.

Prārthanā

(Prayer)

nānyāspṛhā raghu-pate hṛdaye'smadiye
satyaṁ-vadāmi ca bhavānakhilāntarātmā
bhaktiṁ prayacha raghu-puṁgavanirbharāṁ me
kāmādi dōṣarahitaṁ kurumānasaṁ ca
(Tulasī Rāmayaṇ)

This night, O Amma, this daughter is praying to you for real devotion. Kindly make my heart free of the great foes of worldly distraction, anger and greed. Nothing else must I crave. You know this prayer is coming from my heart.

vārāṇasī tīrtthaṅgaḷil
kailās śikhiraṅgaḷiluṁ
ennelleṅguṁ śivamayaṁ tān
ennumuḷkkōvil naṭa turannāl

Amma, who is my heart of hearts, let me open the shrine of my heart and have darśan of your divine form. You are everywhere, not only in Varanāsi and Kailāsa, for those who strive to see you residing in the heart always. Amma, be graceful to hear the prayers of your children.

|| oṁ amṛteśvaryai namaḥ ||

Mēṭam 29, May 12

Praṇāmaṁ

(Prostration)

oṁ kāñcī candraka mañjīra vamśī śobhi svabhūdṛśe
amṛteśvaryai namo namaḥ
amṛteśvaryai namo namaḥ

O Amma, you were immersed in Bhagavān Kṛṣṇa's thoughts always. In your childhood Śrī Kṛṣṇa appeared to you in his yellow robe, peacock feathers, reed flute and various ornaments. Kindly grant me mental strength to strive for a good life and to reach God.

Prabodhanaṁ

(Awakening)

śrī nāthe jānakī nāthe abhedaḥ paramātmani
tathāpi mama sarvasvaṁ
rāmaḥ kamalalōcana
(Tulasī Rāmayaṇ)

Amma says:

"Śrī Hanumān in the attitude of a servant of Śrī Rāma is praying for one-pointed devotion for God in Śrī Rāma's form though he was aware of the fact that all forms are of the same supreme truth. O my children, today all of you listen to this prayer. Many who pray to God do so not for devotion. Those who start to be devotees may deviate after awhile if their wishes are not fulfilled. Quite a few change their mode of worship. Those who had sandal paste on their foreheads as those of Vaiṣṇava devotees suddenly start putting red kuṁkum tilak, as Divine Mother's devotees do. 'No tilak hereafter,' they may think. Many change the form in their photographs and the center of worship. Those who were temple worshippers sometimes leave temples and go to worship in churches and mosques. To change the external mode of worship does not bring the desired effect. You may study different spiritual teachings, learning and accepting the truth in them, yet it is better to stick to one mode of worship.

"Have you heard the story of one devotee named Pākkanār and his brother? One day Pākkanār, who was supposed to be a born low-caste, visited his elder brother who was a born Brahmin. Pākkanār had the innate tendency of correct worship whereas his brother was a ritualistic worshipper. In the morning his brother was performing homas in the names of various deities. When he finished each homa, Pākkanār dug a hole in the ground. He made a lot of holes before his brother's worship was over. When his brother greeted him after his worship, he found many new holes in the ground where Pākkanār was seated. By enquiry, he found that Pākkanār was trying to dig a well. Pākkanār was demonstrating the futility of too many modes of worship, because rituals and various religions actually are meant to gain one-pointed devotion to God by concentration of mind.

"My children, you want to reach your goal, do you not? To stick to one name and form of God is the way. Don't fall prey to your mental distractions. Many who come to you as so-called saviors are equally or more blind. Tell them to leave you alone. Listen to your inner voice purified by the great divine saints with mental instructions.

"These great ones you depend on and advance. Amma never tells anyone to follow her. You stick to the faith you find fit for you and reach full realization in that faith. May all of you enjoy peace and bliss."

Prayatnaṁ

(Practice)

Amma's all-renouncing disciples were sent to serve the public by Amma through various āśraṁ branches. Līla mōḷ, now known by the name Swāminī Ātmaprāṇā, experienced the following:

One day a devotee was talking about his sister in great despair. Swāminī told him if possible to bring her to the āśram. After a while, she came to the āśram on a very busy day. The āśramites were working all day and had no time to prepare the usual meals. So, they shared some kañji and coconut chutney as their breakfast and lunch together. They were about to have this simple meal when the lady arrived. She appeared to be elegant and cheerful. She enjoyed a simple meal served by Swāminī with a few of the āśramites. She found Swāminī was staying in a hut on the top of the small āśraṁ building, and she liked it. She was having a wish recently to stay in a hut like the one she found at the āśram. This coincidence gave fullness of confidence to her doubting mind. The negative feelings she had about her own religion were forced on her by some ministers she had met at a "center of healing." Slowly, while she was talking to Swāmini, she opened her heart. She happened to visit the healing center because she was infertile. "I wanted to have a baby, you know." When she said that, Swāmini enquired whether her wish was fulfilled. She answered that she, who was already 55 years old, was pregnant.

Swāmini was a qualified doctor, and she told her she could examine her if she allowed. Naturally then Swamini advised her to get over this delusion that she was pregnant and face reality as such. Then they started having an emotional discussion, sometimes even with tears. She was adamant only for a little while and said only Jesus was true; other gods and ideas of an Absolute Brahman were all false and demonic.

Swāmini agreed with her that Jesus was true and asked what her concept of Jesus was. "Do you agree that Jesus verily is the living force in you?" To which the lady answered positively.

"Suppose you are asleep—do you have the awareness of the name of Jesus in you as though you are with your living force?"

She for the first time could analyze and find that when her mind is not in a waking state, all the names and forms disappear while her inner self was yet awake.

"Do you agree the final truth is that which lives always without any change in time?"

She agreed. She was for the first time convinced that Jesus was one of the many names given to the all-pervading consciousness, which was the inner self.

Then Swāminī told her that she could visit Amma if she liked.

"If the Creator wishes," was her answer.

Swāmini heard that she went to Amma on the following Sunday and stayed in the āśraṁ for a while. After that, she was a changed person. She was starting to be free and unbound. She was happier and slowly she changed to a more scientific spirituality with Amma's graceful guidance.

Pratijñā

(Oath)

To bring light to those in darkness
To bring peace to the frustrated
To bring knowledge to the ignorant
This will be our constant endeavor with Amma's blessing.

Prārthanā

(Prayer)

yaṁ vaidikā mantra-dṛśaḥ purāṇāḥ
indraṁ yamaṁ mātariśvānamāhuḥ
vedāntino'nirvacanīyam-ekaṁ
yaṁ brahma śabdena vinirdiśanti
śaivāyamīśaṁ śiva ityavocan
yaṁ vaiṣṇavā viṣṇuritistuvanti
buddha stathārhan iti bauddha jaināḥ
satśrī akāleti ca sikkasantaḥ
śāsteti kecit kadicit kumāraḥ
svāmitī māteti piteti bhaktyā
yaṁ prārthayantē jagadīśitāraṁ
sa eka eva prabhuradvitīyaḥ
(Aikyamatya Mantra)

The great seers of the Vedas call the eternal truth "Indra and Yama," etc., whom the Vedāntins call "Brahman," whom the Śaivas call "Śiva," and the Vaiṣṇavas call Viṣṇu," whereas some devotees call this truth Kumāra and others "Śāstā" [Lord Ayyappan]. Names such as "the Lord," "the Mother," "the Father," etc, are all for the ruling force of the cosmos, which is the one sole reality.

ētoru śaktiyāl-ellāṁ pravarttippū
ammahā śaktiyāl prēritarāy
kaṇkaḷuṁ kaṇkaḷkku kaṇṇāy manavum-
innennil pravarttippatuṇṭennāluṁ
prēma svarūpiye darśippānāvāte
khinnarāy sarvadā kēṇiṭunnū
kaṇkaḷkku munniliṅgātma prakāśamāy
ammayinnonnu vannettiyeṅkil

Amma, kindly grant me the strength to perceive the truth behind the actions of perceiving and working. My eyes may fail if you do not grant the divine strength for them to see the force of love and mercy.

|| oṁ amṛteśvaryai namaḥ ||

Mēṭam 30 May 13

Praṇāmaṁ

(Prostration)

oṁ sārvatrika hṛṣīkeśa sānniddhya laharī spṛśe
amṛteśvaryai namo namaḥ
amṛteśvaryai namo namaḥ

O Amma, you identified with Śrī Kṛṣṇa in form and formless aspect and could perceive him everywhere and in every sentient and insentient being. As your child I cry and pray to you to give me constant awareness of your supreme nature.

Prabodhanaṁ

(Awakening)

śubhaṁ karotu kalyāṇaṁ
āyurārogya varddhanaṁ
śatru bhīti praṇāśanaṁ
dīpa jōtirnamostute
(Subhāṣitaṁ)

Amma says:

"O my children, in our country, almost all homes during dusk and twilight used to be purified by the hymns and prayers of the family members. The so-called "modernization" has interfered with this all-powerful and simple way of connecting with the divine. Amma urges you to restart the practice never to stop again. This should be the import of our prayers:

"May all be happy and prosper.
May all be long-living and healthy.
May all foes inside and outside disappear.
May all our lives currents flow smoothly and evenly.
May the worship lamp show our way and lead us to our goal.
Our prostrations again and again."

Children: "O Amma, we give our word to you that hereafter we will start again our good practices. But why should people light a lamp to the photographs of someone who is still alive? We do not agree with it whoever the person may be."

Amma: "Amma cannot understand you, my children. Why so? Is God not in everyone living? Why then should one be dead to be godly?"

Children: "Amma, we just repeat what others say without giving much thought, just making noise as empty vessels do. Kindly give us the real understanding."

Prayatnaṁ

(Practice)

Līla mōḷ remembers a story:

It was soon after Amma's 50th birthday celebrations. A well-known artist and art director of many internationally known Malayāḷaṁ movies happened to see a sign on the wayside with Amma's divine likeness. He wanted to take this sign after the celebrations were over, and the picture was handed over to him. He artistically remolded it, and kept it on the wall of the porch of his house. Later the artist was performing the evening pūjā at his home. While the evening lamp was being lit, he did not perform ārati to Amma's photo. This attracted the attention of a family friend present at that time, who asked him why. The artist told him that he was against worshipping living people. He said, "I don't think it's correct to perform ārati to photographs of living personalities. But I am not at all reluctant in praying to Amma, especially now that I am alone after my wife's death and I have become a 'good boy' free of my bad habits of smoking and drinking."

His friend replied, "I once held a similar view. But something happened to me once in Kuwait that changed my thinking. At that time I had no faith in Amma's greatness, yet I occasionally would assist to help with the good social activities in connection with Amma's work. I once was requested by the organizers to help sponsor a public program in connection with the visit of one of Amma's disciples. I helped in whatever way I could, but thereafter decided not to have any more contact. But can we escape Amma? Swāmiji came and went, and the matter altogether disappeared from my mind. However, the organizers of the regular satsang continued to invite me to attend, but I always avoided doing so.

"Then, one night, when I was driving back from work, a vehicle happened to stop short, blocking my way. I suddenly turned to avoid rear-ending the vehicle. When I stopped, I realized that this had happened right in front of the place where the satsang was to be held. So, I naturally went there.

"What I saw when I entered the hall was a huge oil lamp with seven lighted wicks in front of Amma's picture. This irritated me, as I thought it was improper. I was offered a seat by the organizer. I thought I wouldn't look at the picture. I turned my head to the side. The group was chanting holy names and soon started singing bhajans. Suddenly I felt as if a bomb had exploded in my chest. I felt severe chest pain, headache and my eyes continuously watered. Soon my face automatically turned in the direction of Amma's picture. I again turned my head away, but as if someone were turning it forcefully, my head returned to face the photo. This repeated until my head was fixed in line with the lamp and the photo. I couldn't move my head, which was aching severely. The heaviness in the chest was unbearable, and the watering of my eyes was not stopping. I thought death was fast approaching.

"First I felt irritated and totally angry with Amma. But what to do? I started praying to Amma. Gradually I began to feel better. This incident changed my life. When my way was blocked, Amma's way opened in front of me. Amma is now my all in all. Now Amma and the light from Amma's lamp illumine my life's path."

Pratijñā

(Oath)

Amma, I will take the oath of putting into
practice your divine instructions.

Prārthanā

(Prayer)

na tatra sūryo bhāti
na candra tārkaṁ
nema vidyuto bhānti
kutoyamagniḥi
tamrva bhāntam
anubhāti sarvaṁ
tasya bhāsā sarvam
idaṁ vibhāti
[Kaṭhopaniṣad, 2-2-15]

In the highest realm of the Supreme, all lights have become dim, including that of the sun and the moon, the lightning and fire. By the light of the Supreme, all become shining.

ētu prakāśattilellāṁ prakāśippū
ā prakāśattin prabhāvattālē
sūryanuṁ candranuṁ nakṣatra jālavuṁ
agniyuṁ minnaluṁ minniṭuṁ
ākayālammatan tatvam veḷivākkān
jōtirgaṇaṅgaḷkkuṁ śaktiyilla
svaprabhayālā mahēśi viḷaṅgavē
sundara suprabhātaṁ viṭaruṁ

Amma, when this day ends let me go to refreshing sleep. Let me wake in the morning which is bright with your light.

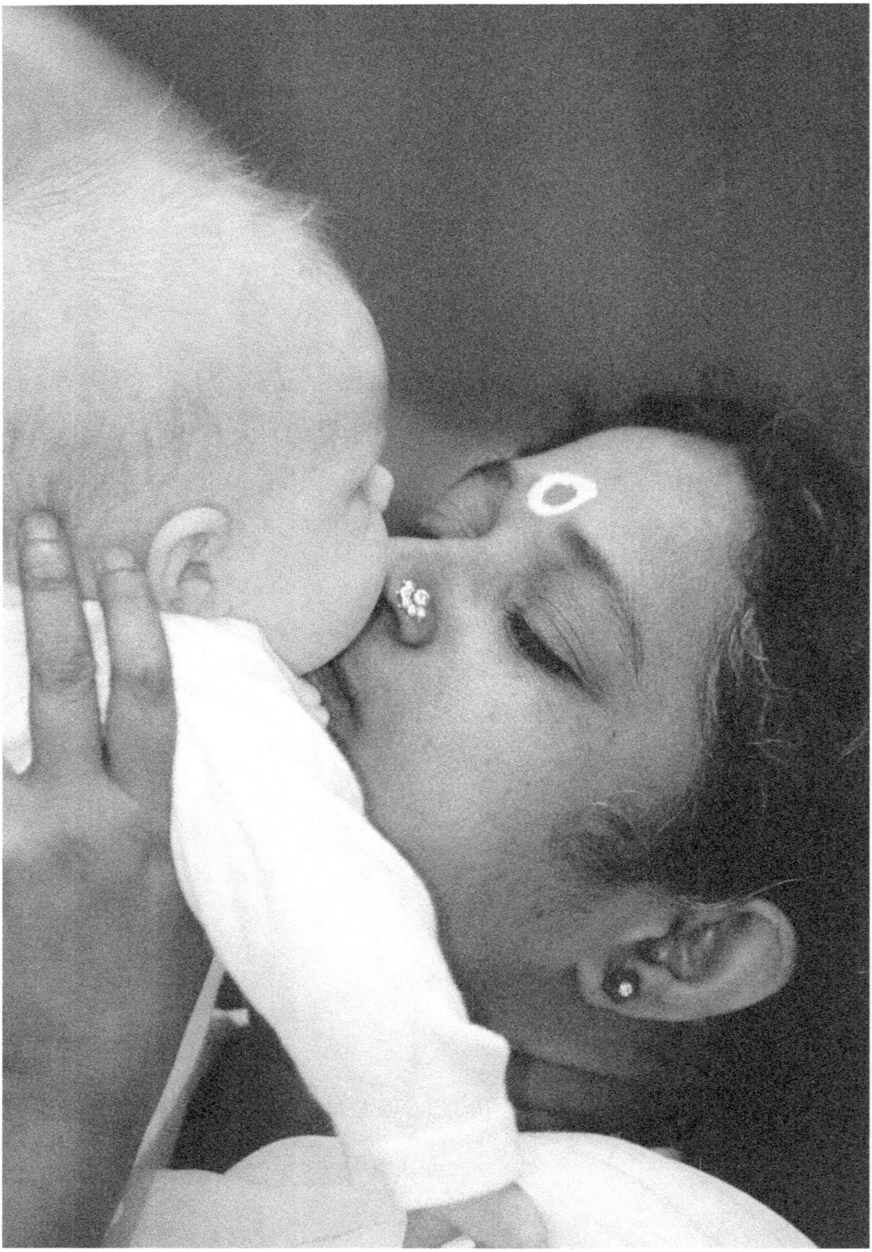

Pronunciation Guide

The letters with dots under them (ṭ, ṭh, ḍ, ḍh, ṇ, ḷ) are palatal consonants; they are pronounced with the tip of the tongue against the hard palate. Letters without such dots are dental consonants and are pronounced with the tongue against the base of the teeth. In general consonants are pronounced with very little aspiration unless immediately followed by an h (kh, gh, th, dh, ph, bh, etc.), in which case aspiration is strong.

a like the a in America
ā like the a in father (vowel is extended)
i like the ea in heat
ī like the ee in beet (long vowel)
u like the ui in suit
ū like the oo in pool (long vowel)
e like the a in gate (long and short in Malayālaṁ, always long in Sanskrit)
o like the o in opinion (long and short in Malayālaṁ, always long in Sanskrit)
ai like the ai in aisle
au like the ow in how
ṛ like the ri in river (usually not rolled)

kh like the kh in bunkhouse (hard aspiration)
gh like the gh in loghouse (hard aspiration)
ṅ like the n in sing
c like the c in cello
ch like the ch in charm (hard aspiration)
jh like the j in just (hard aspiration)
ñ like the ny in canyon
th like the t in table (hard aspiration, tongue at base of teeth)
dh like the dh in redhead (hard aspiration, tongue at base of teeth)

ph like the ph in shepherd or like the f in fun
bh like the bh in clubhouse
v like the v in victory (but closer to a w)
ś like the ci in efficient
ṣ like the sh in shut
ḥ echoes preceding vowel

www.ingramcontent.com/pod-product-compliance
Lightning Source LLC
LaVergne TN
LVHW051737080426
835511LV00018B/3118
* 9 7 8 1 6 8 0 3 7 2 8 1 6 *